PRAISE FOR *THE S.......*

The world of business will benefit from Greg's work by helping those of us who are in leadership positions to understand that starting with people as humans and creating a space for them to be will get the long term fiduciary results we need. Greg gets to the core that we have a responsibility for those in our charge and when we start with them first and help them understand where they have agency the outcomes will come.

I have had the great pleasure of working with Greg and bringing him in to two companies and multiple teams; he brought what he brings in this book. The end results have been an increase in engagement, retention and ultimately productivity. The results in all aspects have been so successful that people who have moved to other teams and/or companies then ask Greg to come work with them. This is the wisdom you will find in *The Strategic Stop*.

Tina L. Dao, MBA, Chief-of-Staff to EVP Engineering &
Head of Engineering Business Operations, Fitbit

The Strategic Stop is a must read for busy professionals, executives, skilled and unskilled workers alike. In fact, this book should be mandatory reading in every high school in America, so that we can train our next generation of leaders how to avoid the traps and pitfalls of selling their souls to the marketplace to the detriment of their own wellbeing. Reading this book will literally cause you to stop dead in your tracks and question how you are living life. It will cause you to rethink, reevaluate, recalibrate, and reassign all the important priorities in your life, bringing them into line with the core essence of your being. Greg's book is refreshing, revitalizing, and relevant to the realities we are currently facing in our world and in our lives. This is the best book I've read this year and I highly recommend it for anyone who is caught up in the rat race and feeling disconnected from life.

Leigh E. Johnson, Esq., Trial Lawyer,
Trial Consultant & Executive Coach

In *The Strategic Stop*, Dr. Nelson's model shows that the answer lies not in doing more, but in digging deeper to discover our true selves and therein our true contributions to humanity.

As a hospital administrator, I face a daily grind to squeeze every extra ounce of life from our doctors, our nurses, and our patients. Having a guide to redirect them from the hamster wheel to a sustainable path to self-awareness is an incredible gift that I look forward to sharing.

The concept of a strategic stop is reminiscent of a surgical time-out where the entire team comes to a halt, discusses the patient and the procedure, before moving forward with the case. Even this small pause has shown to produce significant improvements in outcomes. How much more could our lives be improved by taking strategic stops in our lives to increase our self-awareness before plunging into the future?

Austin Purkeypile, Vice President of Operations,
East Orlando at Florida Hospital

In a culture that says "Go. Go! GO!", author Greg Nelson says "Stop." And his argument is compelling. Rather than urging a spate of mental coasting, Nelson defines periods of intentional reflection. He describes seven strategies for tapping undiscovered inner resources, setting new goals, and becoming one's own best partner in living a fulfilling life. I have been privileged to observe "up close" as Nelson practiced these strategic stops while navigating significant reinventions in his own life. They work! This is a must read for all who consider taking their foot off the gas and using the brake pedal for its best purposes.

Richard Winn, Ed.D., President, Accrediting Commission
for Community and Junior Colleges

The world of business will benefit from Greg's work by confronting the ramifications of this question: What happens to work culture as more and more of us recognize that ROI (Return on Investment) does not always equal ROL (Return on Life)?

With more than 35% of American labor force participants being Millennials, (Pew Research Center analysis of U.S. Census Bureau data) business can no longer count on attracting and retaining new talent based on the old formulas. Millennials have often shared their unwillingness to sacrifice their off-work time or to make other lifestyle compromises in return for financial compensation. It's been argued that millennials' inclination in this regard relates to them having watched their boomer parents delay happiness in return for career advancement, a worldview they're not willing to buy into for themselves.

With "Strategic Stops" Dr. Greg Nelson offers today's increasingly caffeinated leaders and managers (I'm one of them!) compelling ways to integrate the power of productivity with the power of pausing — to help reclaim human "being" instead of blindly chasing human "doing."

Ayesha Mathews-Wadhwa, Design Director, Carbon Black

We are at the point where information—relevant and excellent information—is infinite. What matters most now is our simple capacity to live, love, and lead a fully human life. Greg Nelson helps you discover and feel that newly simple life already pulsing in you. As a reliable and caring guide, Greg will help you muster your courage to stop, feel your body, access your inner wisdom, and connect with all the help in the world that you need. By the end of the journey, you will double down on being your authentic self and experience new levels of your thriving. That's what happened to me. I emerged from reading this book breathing more deeply, seeing more clearly, and making my very next steps more playfully.

Samir Selmanovic, Ph.D., PCC, Transitions Coach,
Organizational Ally, and Retreat Leader,
www.wisdomworkroom.com

This is a must-read as Greg Nelson takes us through the journey of our everyday busy lives. He proves why it is essential to take a "Strategic Stop" for one's personal well-being, the benefits of clearing your mind, and how this can carry over into making you a more successful leader.

With my daily demands of managing the operations of a large organization, I am seeing more and more the significance, as Greg Nelson demonstrates, of disconnecting and prioritizing time to reflect and refuel. I highly recommend this book in becoming a better leader not only professionally, but personally as well. The super power of *The Strategic Stop* will literally stop you in your tracks and make you reevaluate your life for the better.

David Quilleon, Senior Vice President, Global Mission,
State Development & Operations, Best Buddies International

The Strategic Stop is a novel and necessary read for those looking to bring thoughtful order to the chaos of their lives. Each chapter brings wisdom, experience, and a framework for recognizing and utilizing the strategic stop. Greg's book is an essential read which will remain a staple in my library of self-help books.

Cassandra Fale, BSN RN, Yoga Instructor, Industrial and Organizational Psychology Graduate Student

As an engineering leader I have seen time and time again that being thoughtful, calm and deliberate delivers higher quality and faster projects every time. Rushing to meet deadlines creates mistakes, that can end up taking longer to fix than doing it right the first time.

And as a dad, observing the stress and pressure of growing up in a constantly connected world, I couldn't agree more with Dr. Greg's philosophy. It's inspiring to be reminded that both higher performance and less stress can come from an intentional approach to life.

Sam Bowen, Head of Hardware, Tonal

You need to read this book if you feel trapped in nonstop busyness. Dr. Greg Nelson eloquently describes how our current culture is failing us - personally and in organizations - and invites us into another way of being by leveraging strategic stops. Dr. Nelson helps us imagine and implement cycles of rest and renewal in our lives. Taking time out helps us reconnect with what is most important - as individuals and as a team - so we can return to our lives and work with renewed perspective, meaning, and commitment. In these times when being busy can be seen as a badge of honor, Dr. Nelson points the way to caring for ourselves and our teams so we can live and work in an authentic, intentional way, one that supports us in expressing the full potential of this life.

Nancy Larocca Hedley, Founder & CEO, Illumine Coaching & Consulting

THE
STRATEGIC
STOP

*Taking Back Your Life in a
World Obsessed with Busyness*

Gregory P. Nelson, DMin
*Professional Keynote Speaker, Author, and
Team and Leadership Strengths Coach*

The Strategic Stop: Taking Back Your Life
in a World Obsessed with Busyness
Copyright © 2019 by Gregory P. Nelson, DMin

Ballast Press
P. O. Box 330155
San Francisco, CA 94133

Printed in the United States of America

Editing by Lauren Bongard Schwarz
Book design by Carla Green

Paperback ISBN 978-1-7336289-0-7
Ebook ISBN 978-1-7336289-1-4

To Dante

My first grandchild. With your whole life still in front of you, you
will one day be in the workplace to both receive and contribute.
May you find it a place of deep humanity and well-being where
you can be fully alive as you give your very best.

To Shasta

My wife who models so beautifully and powerfully what it means
to live purposefully. Your love and passion, shared with such
exuberance, wisdom, and generosity, have transformed my life and
vision into the human being I am today.

Contents

The Prophecy of the Eagle and the Condor

There is an ancient prophecy told by indigenous people of various cultures around the world. South American tribal elders have called it the Prophecy of the Eagle and the Condor.[1] It is about an ultimate collaboration between ways of life and ways of thinking about the world that must happen for the world's survival. According to tribal leaders, this prophecy has been pointing to its fulfillment in our current human era.

The story says that in the beginning all of Earth's people were as one, but that long ago they divided into two groups that each followed a different path of development. The people of the eagle are highly intellectual, scientific, explorers, adventurers, and conquerors, paying attention to a rational and pragmatic view of the world. They represent the industrial and the masculine. They push the edges of knowledge, information, and technology and end up amassing great material wealth. But it all comes at the expense of their souls and inner spirits, leading to a kind of spiritual impoverishment.

The people of the condor are Earth-based, revolving around the heart, the spirit, the senses, and an intimate connection to the natural world. They develop great intuitive skills based upon their ancient wisdom and understanding of the interconnectedness of all life and all the great cycles of the Earth and the feminine. But this lifestyle and way of being ultimately lead to an impoverishment regarding scientific knowledge and technology, and therefore a disadvantage in the broader material world that threaten to bring their culture to the edge of extinction.

According to the prophecy, the eagle and the condor will ultimately not survive unless they reconnect and initiate significant collaboration between them—in which they bring their unique skills, knowledge, wisdom, and ways of living to each other. When the eagle and the condor begin to fly together, wing to wing, the world will be at one again and life will be brought to a place of sustainability for everyone.

Why Have I Written This Book?

As prophesied, the human family today is at this turning point. Our Western culture is caught up in the never-ending cycle of the obsessive pursuit of rationality, power, control, management, technology, knowledge, and conquering the last frontiers in order to put the stamp of ownership on them. This way of life has resulted in a profound disconnect with our inner spirits and souls. We've been co-opted by the rat race of nonstop busyness of the myriad demands on our lives. It feels like a slow death by to-do lists. In our overwhelm, we have this sneaking suspicion that there must be something more to life than being a slave to the urgent.

Our intellectual and technological achievements are indeed impressive. Much of the good we enjoy these days come from them—some diseases have been eradicated, with the potential of more joining the list; life span has increased; the principles of freedom and democracy have been embraced in more countries, contributing to more equality in more societies than ever; the globe has become smaller because of travel and technological inventions like air flight, internet, smartphones, and visual media. The list of benefits is long.

But the question for today's generations is, At what cost? Two thousand years ago, Jesus made a convicting statement, "What should it profit a man if he should gain the whole world but lose his own soul?" Is it worth losing ourselves in the process of succeeding and producing everything we think we need to do?

Similarly, the indigenous prophecy of the eagle and the condor is calling into question today's imbalance. Western culture has been co-opted by human doing. And in the process, it is losing its soul.

We are being called back to our essential humanity—to embrace our identity as human beings, to bring back into balance our masculine and feminine sides. The eagle and the condor must fly together again.

Herman Hesse, the German poet, novelist, painter, and winner of the 1946 Nobel Prize in Literature, put it this way:

"In each one of you there is a hidden being, still in the deep sleep of childhood. Bring it to life! In each one of you there is a call, a will, an impulse of nature, an impulse toward the future, the new, the higher. Let it mature, let it resound, nurture it! Your future is not this or that; it is not money or power, it is not wisdom or success at your trade—your future, your hard, dangerous path is this: to mature and to find Life in yourselves."[2]

In this book I discuss what it takes to reclaim this vital balance between doing and being. If we are completely caught up in running, building, amassing, creating, consuming, and producing, we are scheduling our being side right out of our agendas. Getting it right takes more than simply taking back our weekends—though that would certainly help. Getting it right takes more than simple time management strategies. Getting it right goes far beyond utilizing agile systems in our workplaces.

Getting it right demands valuing and then shaping into our regular lives what I call strategic stops—opportunities to come face to face with our beautiful humanity and learn the art of authenticity, confidence, clarity about identity and purpose, empathy, honor and respect for each other, and innovative collaboration.

Who Am I to Write this Book?

For the last 15 years I have worked as a full-time professional speaker, leadership and team-strengths coach, and author, mostly in the business world. I have been trusted by big brands such as Amazon, Fitbit, Walmart, Lyft, American Express, and the Bill & Melinda Gates Foundation to maximize their leaders and teams.

Working with hundreds of leaders and teams has given me a seat at the table to facilitate strategic stops in which everyone is given opportunity to radically increase self-awareness, relational empathy, and innovative collaboration. I've seen women and men, when given the space and opportunity, make the courageous choice during sessions to be vulnerable, honest, transparent, and show deep levels of respect, honor, and empathy with each other, and then to put it all together effectively in order to partner and collaborate in creative ways.

I've seen the transformation of these work cultures into places of human potential and human beings, not just human doings. And when this happens, it matters to the whole organization.

Prior to this, I spent 20-plus years as a pastor, journeying with people from the cradle to the grave. I learned all about the very human and often messy process of living and dying. And over time, I saw with increasing clarity how living life works best—how we as humans are designed for ways of being that enhance and enliven human existence—learning firsthand the best practices of being human, as it were. And when I stood beside a dying parishioner, holding his or her hand, I never once heard them say to me or to their families, "I wish I had spent more time at the office."

I am speaking from personal experience as a leader, entrepreneur, parent, and grandparent. I, too, have wrestled with the tug between the urgent and the important. I feel the inner turmoil of having to choose priorities, and depending on which ones I choose, experiencing the consequences. Sometimes it has felt good. Other times it hasn't. Sometimes it has worked well, other times it hasn't worked at all. But I continue working to build the healthiest balance in my life through all the ups and downs, ins and outs.

Finally, I have a doctorate in personal and organizational effectiveness. My study, research, and learnings through the years have extremely energized and informed me about how people work and live best; how, when individuals come together in an organization, the culture gets shaped by both individual influence and group shifts, either for good or not so good, depending on how healthy and whole each person is.

I'm extremely grateful for and thankful to the thousands of people in my working life who have trusted me in various capacities to be in their lives. They have invited me into their journeys at various stages of life to be a supportive, encouraging, and guiding presence. They have taught me so much.

This book, *The Strategic Stop*, is the culmination of some of my learnings developed through my career with people and groups.

It's time for the eagle and the condor to fly together, wing to wing, soaring into the heights of human living—in our workplaces, our homes, our culture. This emphasis is what ultimately provides us with the joy, fulfillment, engagement, and groundedness we hunger for deep inside.
I invite you on this journey to have an open mind, a willing spirit, and a bold confidence. I want you to fly. You won't regret it.

INTRODUCTION

Decaffeinating a Caffeinated Culture

Imagine yourself on a train. The train is traveling at a high speed. Everyone onboard is comfortable, enjoying the passing scenery. But then it becomes apparent that the train is nearing an urban area and its speed is not lessening. The train isn't slowing down like it's supposed to. You're becoming concerned. You finally run up to the front car, pounding on the door behind which the engineer sits. "Hey!" you shout. "We're going too fast into the city! Slow it down!"

The door flies open and you notice the engineer looks desperate. "I can't find the brake! Where is it?" he shouts back.

You look around and see the brake handle. "There it is!" you scream. "Pull it! Pull it!"

The engineer tries to pull the lever. It doesn't budge. "It's jammed!" he says. It's stuck at full throttle!

It doesn't take an understanding of physics to know how this is going to end for everyone onboard.

This scenario, say medical and health sciences experts, is like the condition of our society and culture. Our lives are so fast-paced and hectic that we're living in a constant state of stress. We're traveling through life at nonstop, breakneck speeds, with our brakes jammed, leaving little room for stops along the way.

We live in a caffeinated culture, and I'm not referring to drinking too much coffee.

We exist smack dab in the middle of a 24/7, nonstop culture in which people are always plugged in and tuned out. We feel constant pressure that with so much going on in the world we need to stay engaged all the time. So many demands on our lives, so little time to fulfill them all. We live with guilt if we don't.

A 2016 survey from Deloitte found that Americans collectively check their phones eight billion times per day. The average for individual Americans is 46 checks per day, including during leisure time, like watching TV, spending time with friends, and eating dinner.[3]

This constant clamor we're all bombarded with has been labeled by the World Health Organization as a "modern plague."[4] That's a serious designation that deserves serious response. After all, when faced with plagues smart humans always act to mitigate the threat. Right?

Whenever biological plagues invade our world these days, there's an all-out war declared on them: AIDS, Ebola, Zika, the flu, norovirus. Governments band together, collaborating with the brightest minds and best technologies available, to combat and destroy at all costs these threats to humanity.

And yet we're living with a plague that is destroying our very humanity, not to mention the human race. But so many of us aren't concerned enough to change our destructive lifestyles.

In 1859, famous British nurse Florence Nightingale stated that "unnecessary noise is the most cruel absence of care that can be inflicted on the sick or well."[5] Even back then, the constant clamor was inflicting damage on human beings. Sadly, 160 years later, we still haven't learned the lesson. Multiple generations, including ours, have paid and are paying the price for disregard.

The Price of Unmanaged Stress

The good news is that our bodies are designed with systems that respond to stress. Here's the way Dr. Archibald Hart, chair of the Fuller Graduate School of Psychology during my doctoral work, described it:

"When the state of alarm or emergency is triggered, our various physiological systems are bathed in adrenaline, which disrupts normal functioning and produces a heightened state of arousal. In the immediate 'emergency' reaction, the heart beats faster, digestion is speeded up, and a host of hormones is released into the bloodstream to prepare us for dealing with the emergency."[6]

For those moments, we have been equipped with the fight or flight capacity. Our systems see a threat and they kick into gear immediately. Adrenaline gets released, and we are empowered to act and react until the threat is gone.

But here's a kicker: body systems don't know whether the threat is real or simply perceived. Our ancestors opened the front doors of their abodes after a night of sleep not knowing whether they would encounter a ravenous bear or lion. They were on hyperalert.

These days, we walk out the front door not expecting a lion or bear. But we're still feeling a threat—usually in the form of beliefs or perceptions or radical desires. "Will people at work think I'm any good?" "Will my spouse be gone when I get home this evening?" "Will my son get in trouble again at school? Will I get a call from the principal?" "Will I make my project deadline at work?" "Am I ready for my boardroom presentation to the executives or to my board members?" "Will my paycheck be enough this month to pay our bills?" "Why isn't my best friend returning my calls? She must not think I'm worth it anymore. Have I done something to displease her or make her think less of me?"

We live every day with hyper stress, sometimes real and other times perceived. Our brains don't immediately distinguish between the two. As a result, our systems are running rampant with an overload of adrenaline, which is constantly over-stimulating our bodies and mental systems. And no system is designed to work at maximum capacity all the time, continuously, full-throttle with the brake jammed. Something is going to break down.

And here's another kicker: the same physiological response kicks in even when we're experiencing positive stress—doing things we enjoy and really want to do. Our systems become infused with adrenaline during these activities as well. The thrill of excitement produces the same response as the fear of danger.

> No system is designed to work at maximum capacity all the time, continuously, full-throttle with the brake jammed. Something is going to break down.

This is why some people are addicted to living on the edge and have a constant need for excitement, action, adventure, and risk. The activities themselves aren't the problem. People are having a great time. The problem is they're actually addicted to the adrenaline that makes them feel high in those moments. So they never want to slow down. They want to keep going.

Dr. Hart summarizes the point of all of this: "Anything—pleasant or unpleasant—that arouses your adrenaline system and mobilizes your body for 'fight or flight,' then doesn't let up and allow time for recovery can predispose you to stress disease. Your body simply adapts to living in a constant state of emergency—and you feel no discomfort until damaging results occur."[7]

Unmanaged stress is at epidemic levels. And it's creating havoc on the quality of life for human beings everywhere. It's time for us to consciously develop a smarter, more strategic plan.

The Secret that High-Performing Athletes Know

My oldest son, Vaughn, is an Ironman multiple times over. His latest feat was competing in Kona, the Ironman World Championships. The whole family was there to cheer him on.

You can imagine the dedication, commitment, and training it takes to compete on this level (much less to even finish these events). I am in total awe of him! And, needless to say, extremely proud.

In conversation with him after this race, I was commenting about how impressed I was with his amazing dedication and training levels. And that's when he told me a truth that stunned me: in actuality, all the powerful effects of the hours of physiological training only benefit your body during recovery times.

Let that sink in for a moment. You can train 24/7 to build up your cardio, muscular, nutritional, and psychological strength, but it's only during recovery times that your hard work actually has an impact.

The human system is designed to achieve homeostasis—a return to powerful equilibrium and total alignment with all parts that then produces a maximized existence—within recovery times. We are physiologically shaped to enhance well-being via intentional, strategic pauses.

I call this the strategic stop. It is an intentional decision to take a break from our typical fast pace of life. It's a choice to stop—a purposeful pause. And it's strategic when it's a choice to stop for the purpose of engaging in something that facilitates recovery to a state of equilibrium for our bodily, emotional, relational, and even organizational systems.

What Does a Strategic Stop Look Like?

Here are some illustrations of what a strategic stop can look like for us. In the next nine chapters, I'll get into more detail about several of these and why they matter in optimizing our human systems.

- Choosing to have your teams come together for team sessions (in off-site or on-site team retreats or executive half-days). The purpose? To reconnect with each other and not just report progress; to stop the busyness in order to refocus; to build a sense of team identity in which each person is recognized for their value, strengths, and unique differences. Your teams and leaders desperately need strategic stops, too!
- Taking a few minutes of personal pause and quiet for meditation, mindfulness, breathing, and expressions of gratitude.
- Going on a personal retreat for a day or weekend.
- Engaging in a weekly sabbath (a Hebrew word meaning "rest," "pause," "to cease"), during which you unplug from technology and consumerism in order to re-center yourself in what and who matters most to you.
- A walk during which you simply observe what's around you or have a meaningful conversation with a partner or friend.
- Regularly unplugging your electronics for an hour or day. Silence creates more brain cells.
- Getting 7–9 hours of sleep every night.
- Going on a date night (and being unplugged during it!).
- Family night with the kids and parents together. Having fun, playing, reading, singing, engaging in volunteer activities, or simply hanging out and watching a great TV show or movie together.
- A coaching or therapy session to reflect on your life and what's working or not working.
- Yoga, exercise, or massage.
- Time for journaling.
- Playing games with friends.
- Savoring food and drink at a cafe (emphasis on savoring).

The list can be creatively endless.

The point is, a strategic stop is about you being more intentional about the kind of life you want to live—both at work and at home. You are refusing to allow the urgent to dictate your choices and priorities. You are in charge. You are not the victim of your life and schedule, even though you might think you are because someone else always seems to have authority over what you do and when you do it.

The strategic stop is you taking back your life in order to really live your life. And that choice radically impacts for good your team, your leaders, your family, and your friends—everyone around you.

> The strategic stop is you taking back your life in order to really live your life.

In 1948, only a year after the word *workaholic* was coined in Canada, the German philosopher Josef Pieper wrote these words about the purpose of stopping in the midst of our work-centric culture:

"Leisure is not justified in making the functionary as 'trouble-free' in operation as possible, with minimum 'downtime,' but rather in keeping the functionary human ... and this means that the human being does not disappear into the parceled-out world of his limited work-a-day function, but instead remains capable of taking in the world as a whole, and thereby to realize himself as a being who is oriented toward the whole of existence.

"This is why the ability to be 'at leisure' is one of the basic powers of the human soul. The power to be at leisure is the power to step beyond the working world and win contact with those superhuman, life-giving forces that can send us, renewed and alive again, into the busy world of work."[8]

This is why, in this book, I describe nine power pauses—strategic stops—that serve as significant ways to ignite and re-ignite your human-being side of life, leadership, and the groups of people you work and live with. These nine strategies are vital ways to reclaim your holistic humanity and build an existence that has meaning, value, and vitality.

Could you use more of those three qualities in your life these days—meaning, value, and vitality? I don't know of many people who couldn't. We all have a lot of things that are draining energy from us. We can't avoid all of them. But we can avoid many. These chapters will help you find ways to recapture vital energy in the most important areas of your life.

If you're a leader who manages teams, a CEO who heads up an entire organization, or a human-resources leader in charge of employee engagement and leadership development, this book is for you. It will help guide you to pay attention to the aspects of leadership and employee engagement that are proven to transform the culture of your people and increase your ultimate purpose. It will help you reclaim more humanity in the workplace, where people can be human beings and not just human doings. You cannot do all of that without strategic stops.

If you're a busy person, no matter what roles you have personally and professionally, this is a guidebook for how to not only survive, but especially how to thrive in your world. It will lead you into intentional pauses that will help you reclaim your full humanity, even in the midst of the whirlwind of life. If you're needing more margin in your day-to-day experience, this will shape how you can utilize that margin in ways that will empower you to achieve your fullest human potential.

My hope is that by reading this book you will feel challenged, inspired, motivated, and informed about how you can shape your most fulfilling and satisfying life and work. At the end of each chapter there are sections for personal and team application to help you transform your human doing into human being. I encourage you to take time to utilize these resources.

Remember, this good life—a life where you feel fully alive, a life of well-being—doesn't simply fall from the sky to encompass you. You are the steward of your life. And it is your responsibility and joyful privilege to help shape it with intention and purpose.

So why do we so rarely make this strategic choice to stop along the way?

Start With Rest

The Power of Sleep

Ever since I've been wearing my Fitbit tracker, I've been able to keep close eye on my sleeping patterns. It informs me how often I awake during the night and what percentage of my sleep is light, REM, and deep. It gives me a comparison with my previous nights' sleep. And it tells me how my sleep patterns compare with those of other men my age.

It has really increased my level of awareness about my sleep habits, needs, and goals. So when I don't get eight hours (my nightly target), I can evaluate what I did that evening that might have impacted my sleep patterns. I've been able to be smarter about my day and evening choices that enhance and detract from a good night's sleep.

Sleep is the original strategic stop that helps accomplish the physiological and psychological restoration our human systems need. "Sleep provides an opportunity for the body to repair and rejuvenate itself. Many of the major restorative functions in the body like muscle growth, tissue repair, protein synthesis, and growth hormone release occur mostly, or in some cases only, during sleep."[9]

The quantity and quality of sleep we get have profound impacts on our brains' abilities for learning and memory. In sleep, our brains "clean out toxins, process the day's experiences, and sometimes work on problems that have been occupying our waking minds."[10]

And look what happens when we don't get enough sleep. "Being chronically tired to the point of fatigue or exhaustion means that we are less likely to perform well. Neurons do not fire optimally, muscles are not rested, and the body's organ systems are not synchronized."[11]

I've done work in many different kinds of organizations, including major corporations, and whenever I meet one on one with leaders and team members I ask them about their sleep patterns. It's staggering how many of them talk about not sleeping well or enough. Many skip sleep for the purpose of doing more work. Others sleep far less than the optimum. All of them feel the pressure to keep up with the many demands of work. And they openly talk to me about the negative consequences they're experiencing.

Arianna Huffington, in her profound book *The Sleep Revolution*, makes the observation, "Today, so many of us fall into this trap of sacrificing sleep in the name of productivity. But, ironically, our loss of sleep, despite the extra hours we put in at work, adds up to more than eleven days of lost productivity per year per worker, or about $2,280. This results in a total annual cost of sleep deprivation to the US economy of more than $63 billion, in the form of absenteeism and presenteeism (when employees are present at work physically but not really mentally focused)."[12]

Contrary to popular opinion, sleep isn't just some luxury for those who have the time and leisure. It's not an experience that the high performers and uber-productive people in our midst can simply choose to neglect or cut corners on. Sleep as the original strategic stop is a fundamental and vital aspect of maintaining necessary human resilience.

Neglect it and you and those around you pay the price!

A Creation Poem About Optimum Design

One of the ancient Hebrew creation poems[13] has the divine creator forming and shaping the first human from the earth—a dirt statue lying motionless on the ground. And then the creator breathes the divine breath into it and it comes to life—fully alive. Awake. Notice the progression. Sleep precedes awakeness.

When it comes time to create the next human, the divine creator causes the person to fall asleep again. This time, the creator takes a rib from this first person and uses it to shape and build the next human. Once again the divine breath produces life. They both wake up from sleep. And together they are fully alive. Same progression. Sleep. Awake.

One of the transformational paradigms in this ancient poem is that this cycle of sleep and awakeness is built into the very creative design of human life. Sleep. Awake. Sleep. Awake. Indeed, the poem paints this entire design into all of earthly creation. "And there was evening, and there was morning. Day four."[14] Evening. Sleep. Morning. Awake. Next day. Evening. Sleep. Morning. Awake. Next day.

> When I choose to go to sleep, I am laying aside my drive to be the master of my world. Instead I let myself go to a place where I cannot control anything. I release my need to control. I allow myself to simply be. Asleep.

Another profound implication of this natural cycle is that when we choose to sleep we are embracing a fundamental truth about what it means to be human—life is not exclusively about productivity, production, and consumption. It's also about receiving, trusting stillness, contentment, and gratitude.

When I choose to go to sleep, I am laying aside my drive to be the master of my world. Instead I let myself go to a place where I cannot control anything. I release my need to control. I allow myself to simply be. Asleep.

In this way, sleep becomes a strategic stop to empower me to become more fully human and, therefore, more fully alive.

Befriending Silence

Ongoing research shows that our brains actually create more brain cells when we stop and engage in silence.[15]

A researcher at Duke University examined the effect of noise on the brains of mice. She used silence as a control between the tests.

Groups of mice were subjected to different types of sounds: music, white noise, and calls from baby mice. The fourth group was the control group and received two hours of silence.

The first three groups experienced positive neurological results, but they were temporary. The fourth group, which had listened to two hours of silence, experienced the most significant neurological changes—their brains actually created new cells in the hippocampus area, which has the capacity for creating new memories.

And what's more, these new cells turned into neurons. "Silence is really helping the new generated cells to differentiate into neurons and integrate into the system," thus revealing a connection between silence and neurogenesis.[16]

The danger of nonstop sound and noise in our daily existence and normal rhythms of living is that we are inhibiting our brains from developing new neuronal pathways that can contribute to new learning, curiosity, and meaningful connections with our world. Lack of silence is a killer.

So one has to stop and ask important questions: Where do I experience silence in my life? Am I surrounding myself with constant noise and never allowing times of silence?

There have been times I've begun a team coaching session with a moment of silence. I've asked the group to pause, close their eyes, and take some deep breaths to help everyone slow down internally and externally. You can actually feel the atmosphere relax, the normal tensions of busyness ebbing away, and everyone becoming fully present to the moment.

I've talked to many people who, when I probe their reasons for lack of intentional silence, tell me that silence makes them uncomfortable. "Why?" I ask. "Because silence forces me to think more, to reflect," some have told me. "I'm afraid of what might suddenly come to mind during silence." Or, "I just can't keep my brain from shouting back at me. Silence is almost impossible." So, in essence, they resist silence in order to keep from facing painful things. Noise is easier. It's a distraction.

In 2006, Luciano Bernardi was studying the impact of music on physiology. His query: Do varying types of music impact people's physical responses differently? And how?

He of course discovered that different musical styles did affect blood pressure, heart rate, and circulation on the brain. Slower music reduced those symptoms.

But what he didn't anticipate was the results on the participants of the silent pauses between the music tracks.

Those "periods of silence inserted between tracks of music were much more relaxing than the soundtracks designed to induce relaxation or periods of silence administered without music in between. Physiologically, taking a 'silence break' had the most profound relaxing and calming effect."[17]

So it turns out that stopping is truly strategic, even when it means stopping to be silent and nothing else. Silence not only allows our bodies and brains to rest, it also allows the adrenaline to drain from our systems in healthy and restorative ways.

Go figure.

In this day and age, even though the noise and chaos are more aggressive and invasive than ever before, we also have the technology and choice to leverage that technology to shut out this undue stimulation.

Here are some simple suggestions for how to take mini-strategic stops for silence or more quiet rest at work or while out and about:

"Alex Doman, coauthor of *Healing at the Speed of Sound*, recommends taking two five-to 10-minute 'quiet breaks' a day: Close your office door, walk to an isolated park bench, or even sit in a bathroom stall while wearing noise-canceling headphones (not ones that are playing music, even if it is Brahms' lullaby). This will give your body a rest from noise-induced stress responses and help fend off disease down the road. It also allows your brain time to process all the stimuli it has encountered."[18]

So why is it that we allow ourselves to feel so pressured to be plugged in all the time? To feel guilty when we're not working or being productive or getting all our to-do lists done? Why do we drive ourselves incessantly?

Every Indy 500 driver knows that this premier auto-racing competition can never be completed, all 500 laps around the 2.5-mile oval track, without strategically chosen pit stops. They simply don't have enough fuel or tire tread to go nonstop for that complete distance.

Strategic stops.

You cannot make it nonstop either, no matter how much you try to convince yourself you can. By trying, you're robbing yourself of the very tool you need to restore, renew, revitalize, and reboot. You become more susceptible to being overcome by information smog.

You need a detox of the mind and body.

Strategic stops.

Why We Don't Stop for Rest More Often

The question is, are you structuring your life to encompass strategic stops? If so, what works for you? If not, why aren't you? What belief is driving you to go nonstop? How can you change that limiting belief?

If we are really honest with ourselves, we have to admit that there are certain beliefs we maintain consciously or unconsciously that drive our choices and priorities toward workaholism.

Like what?

Perhaps it's a picture of identity that you aren't valuable or worth as much if you don't produce everything that you think you're supposed to or that others expect of you.

Perhaps it's the fear that if you're not working as many hours as your manager or leader or other high performers around you, you'll be labeled as lazy or unproductive. So better make sure you're not only staying as late or later, but that you're also always available by email or text on the weekends or on vacations.

Perhaps you feel that you're not as competent as those around you. So you compensate by working harder and longer.

Perhaps you're a very self-motivated person. You have no problem pushing yourself. But because you lean toward being perfectionistic, you simply refuse to stop working on your tasks until you get it just right. So you put in longer hours—whatever it takes to achieve the standard you're striving for.

Perhaps you feel the social pressure of producing, working, and getting involved in everything. You're surrounded by people who have the expectation that everyone contributes by putting in longer and longer hours. Social status goes up the more you're involved in. You're afraid they'll think less of you if you don't join them.

One of the factors that makes this so difficult for all of us is that we live in a culture that celebrates these behaviors. One psychologist describes it this way: "These are traits that seem to be celebrated in many ways in modern American culture. For example, many cultural heroes of popular TV shows, particularly those shows that portray the lives of doctors, lawyers and successful business people, are hard-driving individuals who seem to have no life other than work. What each shares is a grandiose sense of his or her own self-importance that is central to the definition of narcissism."[19]

Ouch. But that's a perspective we have to pay careful attention to as we evaluate our choices and priorities.

I remember pastoring at a private boarding school campus where the principal operated in this way. He could always be seen sitting at his desk, working away at all hours of the night. He was quick to tell his staff that he didn't expect them to keep the same hours. But I had numerous conversations with staff who expressed feeling deep pressure to match his choices. They felt like they were not going to be as valued unless they put in the time as well.

It's true, his modeling spoke louder than his words. And yet, at the same time, many allowed themselves, in spite of his permission-giving words, to feel deep internal pressure to overwork.

So I asked some of the staff these questions: "Why do you feel this internal pressure? Where is this pressure coming from in your mind and heart? What limiting beliefs might your feeling of pressure be an expression for? What is the principal's behavior triggering in you?"

Many of these questions invite us to try to understand the underlying beliefs that drive our behaviors. I'll discuss this challenge in chapters Three and Four, Strengthening Self-Awareness and Shifting Limiting Beliefs.

Summoning the Courage to Rest

I was on an evening walk after work when I came upon a scene halfway up Telegraph Hill. I'd seen this vista many times before, but this time I was struck by its beauty—San Francisco Bay dotted with the white sails of sailboats, the Bay Bridge, blue sky, trees in the foreground, hills in the distance, and a huge cruise ship docked at the SF Terminal not far below me. I stood there taking in the vista, just letting my mind daydream about anything I noticed and saw right then. After about five minutes of letting my mind go wherever it wanted, I walked on...actually feeling quite energized.

There's a wonderful article in the New York Times[20] about this mental process that so often gets ignored or demeaned because our culture puts priority on busyness and productivity. Being busy all the time is being used as a badge of honor these days—"I'm so busy because I am just so important." When is the last time a colleague called you on the phone and said, "Hey, what's up?" And you responded, "I am right in the middle of doing nothing. Can I call you back?"

> Being busy all the time is being used as a badge of honor these days—"I'm so busy because I am just so important."

Daydreaming—doing nothing—is seen as lazy, nonproductive, and a waste of time when there's so much that needs to be done. In fact, many people grew up with the old saying, "Idleness is the Devil's playground."

The Dutch actually have a word for this experience of doing nothing— *niksen*. It's essentially about stopping, pausing, in order to let your mind wander, like gazing out a window, or simply looking out over a scene like I did without any agenda in mind. It's about giving your brain a rest.

Psychologists have picked up this word and are using it as a prescription for mental health and well-being. Research has found that "daydreaming—an inevitable effect of idleness—literally makes us more creative, better at problem-solving, better at coming up with creative ideas. Total idleness is required."[21]

As a result of *niksen*, stress levels decline, a sense of calm and peace emerge, and the brain receives new energy.

That's exactly what I experienced on my walk.

This is the significance of building into our lives more strategic stops designed for simply doing nothing—purposeful pauses for daydreaming, a moment of rest to quiet our body systems. It takes courage to allow yourself to do this, doesn't it? It's a bold moment of going against the accepted norm of culture to give ourselves the permission to stop for rest, for simply doing nothing that everyone around us considers so necessary. In taking this simple strategic stop, we help to reshape our culture away from an obsession with busyness to a more human "being" experience.

Adequate rest—whether it's sleep, doing nothing, or silence and quiet—are crucial for our human well-being. We limit those experiences at great peril and disadvantage to our lives.

So I dare you to be bold and take this strategic stop. You just might really enjoy it.

PERSONAL PAUSES

- Identify three specific things you could address in your life to help you get more sleep at night (8–9 hours).

- Plan two 10-minute stops of silence during your work day. What will you do to experience silence during those stops (for example, use noise-canceling headphones, find a more secluded location inside or outside the office, close your office door)?

- Is it difficult for you to rest or withdraw from your busy activities to be in silence? If so, identify what the obstacle to you is. What specific steps might you take to push through that obstacle?

- Challenge yourself to engage in doing nothing. It can be on a walk somewhere or sitting at your desk or at some other location or event. Allow your brain to simply roam with no specific agenda. Take in the present moment based upon what you're observing around you. Let yourself just be.

TEAM PAUSES

⏸ Start a team session with a two minute "close your eyes and breathe deeply" exercise to slow everyone down physically and psychologically before beginning the regular agenda. Be in silence during that time. Then debrief the experience with the group.

⏸ Team sharing questions: "How do you tend to react to silence? Is it comfortable to you or not? Why?"

⏸ Team exploration: "Identify three specific things you could address in your life to help you get more sleep at night (at least eight hours)." Challenge each person to experiment with getting enough sleep for two to three weeks. Have them monitor their feeling of engagement and productivity at work after that time. And then have a session to share with each other what it was like.

Shape Your Recovery

In the middle of my eighth-grade year, my family moved from Japan to Guam. I was extremely sad to leave behind the friends I had gone to school with for most of my elementary years. And yet I was excited for the adventure of living on a tropical island and meeting new friends.

Most likely because I was the new kid in the class, I was elected president. And the biggest task, especially halfway through the year, was to plan our graduation. Other than choosing a speaker for the service, the most important decision was coming up with a class motto.

I remember sitting around a table with the other officers, brainstorming catchy sentences. One of us even had a book of mottos to scrutinize for ideas. After much conversation and some arguing, we landed on the perfect eighth-grade motto we were convinced was completely original (until I discovered later that almost every graduating class all over the world had a form of this motto): "Onward ever, backward never."

Such impressive profundity. Although no one really knew exactly what it meant (and we didn't really care since it sounded cool), we were pretty clear that it was a reminder to just keep pushing forward no matter the obstacles. After all, our parents preached to us this core value—don't give up; keep going; stay with it until you finish it; and if you fall, pick yourself up, put one foot in front of the other, and keep fighting the good fight.

We were celebrated if we never gave up—in sports, scholastics, religious commitment, and relationships. The outcome was in the end more important. When we received an A on an assignment or a test, we were praised for the exceptional grade. It wasn't important that we had to stay up until 3 a.m., studying, working, and losing sleep to be ready. After all, we not only passed, we passed with flying colors. No wonder that ever since we joined the adult workforce we have been equally praised and rewarded for staying up late working on our projects, for being the last one out of the office, for responding to every email from the boss even on weekends and vacations. Always on, always available.

The expectation in our work culture is to push through discomfort and exhaustion in order to get the job done. CEOs continue to foster work environments where employees have to know the answers to their questions; if they don't, after being shamed in front of the group, they're expected to find it and report back, no matter how much time it takes, even after work hours. For many leaders, this is a sign of loyalty to the company and their leadership and a recipe for employee success.

I just read a news report about a huge company in which many of the warehouse employees carry around bottles to use when they need to use the bathroom so that they don't miss their goals by taking time off to go to the restroom. The pressure of productivity is so intense they resort to extreme measures to stay on task.

This, says our culture, is what it means to be resilient. And resilience is a very important value.

Notice all the different idioms people use to describe what is by popular acclaim considered to reflect the experience of resilience:

- Power through it
- Grit your teeth and bear it
- No pain, no gain
- Bounce back
- Pick yourself up, dust yourself off, and keep going
- Hang in there
- Don't give up
- Use your elbow grease
- Stay with it
- Determination
- You can go one more round
- Keep slogging
- When the going gets tough, the tough get going

You get the idea.

Our culture places a high priority on dogged persistence, especially in the face of difficulty, challenges, and obstructions along the way. America was founded on the value of self-determination and rugged individualism. "Keep fighting until the victory is won."

Now, there's certainly nothing wrong with the encouragement to persist. Often it's while pushing through the storms of life that we end up experiencing our greatest and most fulfilling victories. Our inner spirits need to be called to this higher ground.

But as a result of this mono-focus, the true definition of resilience has been tragically skewed.

Here's the way authors Shawn Achor and Michelle Gielan put it: "We often take a militaristic, tough approach to resilience and grit. We imagine a marine slogging through the mud, a boxer going one more round, or a football player picking himself up off the turf for one more play. We believe that the longer we tough it out, the tougher we are, and therefore the more successful we will be. However, this entire conception is scientifically inaccurate."[22]

What they're referring to is the primary definition of *resilience* that comes from biology. It refers to the built-in regulating system called homeostasis. *Homeostasis* is a word coined by Dr. Walter Cannon in 1930 to describe the body's capacity to adjust itself in the midst of various unbalancing conditions back to a place of equilibrium. The word comes from the Greek words for "same" and "steady."

For example, when you get overheated, your body regulates its temperature by producing sweat and perspiration, which cool your body by making more moisture on the skin available for evaporation. It's a fairly common homeostatic phenomenon. On the other hand, the body reduces heat loss by sweating less and reducing blood circulation to the skin. The opposite homeostatic process. The goal in both cases: a return to balance.

Our human systems are designed to regulate themselves by triggering what is called negative feedback—"negative" not as in "bad," but as in "opposite." The goal is to keep balance that helps to facilitate our well-being.

Emeritus professor Kelvin Rodolfo of the University of Illinois at Chicago's Department of Earth and Environmental Sciences illustrates this negative feedback process for maintaining homeostasis:

"We can regard a car and its driver as a unified, complex, homeostatic or 'goal-seeking' system in that it seeks to keep the car moving on track. The driver does not steer by holding the wheel in a fixed position but keeps turning the wheel slightly to the left and right, seeking the wheel positions that will bring the naturally meandering car back on track ... If the car skids, the driver automatically responds by quickly steering in the opposite direction. Such abrupt negative feedback, however, usually over-corrects, causing the car to move toward the other side of the road ... The car and driver recover from the skid by weaving from side to side, swerving a little less each time. In other words, each feedback is less than the last departure from the goal, so the oscillations 'damp out.' Negative feedback takes time and such a time lag is an essential feature of many natural systems. This may set the system to oscillating above and below the equilibrium level."[23]

In other words, resilience actually involves more than simply pushing through obstacles to get to a goal or having the courage to get back up when you are knocked down in order to power ahead. Resilience is about establishing regulation in order to achieve balance—an intentional self-adjusting that involves looking carefully at your current condition and then finding strategic ways to balance that with its opposite in order to come to a place of well-being.

What does this mean in our everyday lives? Let me suggest several implications.

1. Achieving Balance Takes Time and Practice

Notice Dr. Rodolfo says that achieving homeostasis (via resilience) takes time. We can't expect immediate results whereby we act and then the tension is quickly resolved. Considering a negative feedback loop means assessing your current status in order to discover what the opposite condition might be that you can then move toward.

Though your body might do this automatically, your brain needs more thoughtful attention on how to cooperate. It takes practice to figure out how to lessen the tendency to overcorrect or overcompensate.

I remember my dad taking me during winter to a large parking lot where there were no other cars. He had me practice sliding in the snow and then trying to stop the slide. I was scared to death at first. I was grabbing the steering wheel so tightly my knuckles were white and all my muscles tense.

The first number of times, I over-turned the steering wheel and completely spun out. Nothing like doing donuts in the snow without wanting to. I was completely out of control.

But with time and practice, and with increasing confidence, I learned exactly how much to over- or understeer in order to straighten out the car's trajectory, how much to touch the brakes with my foot, and how much to depress the gas pedal. Little by little, all these movements and strategic choices became second nature. As my dad used to tell me, practice makes perfect.

> Resilience is about establishing regulation in order to achieve balance—an intentional self-adjusting that involves looking carefully at your current condition and then finding strategic ways to balance that with its opposite in order to come to a place of well-being.

And then when I actually was driving in the snow on the roads one day, in the stress of the moment, I forgot everything and crashed. Bummer! But that too was a learning experience. I debriefed to determine what I had done wrong or what I could have done better. And the next time, I was better at it.

Achieving balance, engaging our built-in resilience, and leveraging homeostasis in order to enjoy a higher level of well-being simply takes time, practice, and strategic intentionality.

Evaluation is key. If your life feels out of balance these days, take some time to think about it. Ask yourself what behaviors or thinking you might be engaging in that are creating imbalance. Then ask yourself what the opposite response might be. Give yourself that strategic negative feedback. Once you've discovered it, make courageous choices that align with that. And then keep practicing until you get the balance right.

2. Achieving Balance Takes Honesty and Bravery

This isn't easy for any of us. It takes bold honesty to confront our stressors because most of the time those stressors are our personal responses to circumstances. We are afraid to confront our boss, for example, about the demands for overworking. We don't want to appear weak or incompetent or lazy to her or to our peers.

We hesitate to be transparent about our exhaustion to our family and friends because we want to project the image of competency—after all, other people seem to be making it with just as much going on. They seem to be balancing their incessant demands; why can't we?

And we don't want to admit defeat to ourselves because our self-identity is based upon the ability to keep going when things get tough. We're not quitters. We're strong and capable of overcoming anything. We have the Winston Churchill paradigm: "We shall never surrender! Victory at all costs!"

The tragedy is that because of this culturally driven pressure and practice, companies are spending upward of $62 billion a year paying for lost productivity stemming from health and safety consequences of employee exhaustion and stress.[24] And the amount of money that gets spent on personal health care continues to rise every year. We are all paying the price.

True resilience takes courageous honesty. And it takes self-reflection. I'll talk specifically about the necessity of strategic self-reflection in the next chapter.

3. Achieving Balance Takes Smart Choices

Resilience isn't simply about letting things happen as they happen. And it's not about grabbing the wheel of a skidding vehicle and holding on for dear life, hoping it will right itself.

Resilience is about taking command and making informed decisions about how and what it will take to achieve balance. It's looking at the current imbalance and knowing that what you need most is strategic recovery time.

We might admit that we really do need recovery time. It's time that we stop more frequently, we admonish ourselves. But stopping is just the first step.

Many of us have experienced the painful reality of finally falling into bed for some well-deserved and needed sleep, only to find ourselves lying awake in bed for hours thinking about a project at work or some other challenge in our lives. We can't seem to shut off our brains.

Has that ever happened to you?

Apparently, stopping isn't always enough. If we get up in the morning having lain awake all night thinking and planning and even counting jumping sheep, we haven't truly rested like we need. Equilibrium and balance don't come automatically just because we're in bed.

Remember Winnie the Pooh?

"But [Pooh] couldn't sleep. The more he tried to sleep the more he couldn't. He tried counting Sheep, which is sometimes a good way of getting to sleep, and, as that was no good, he tried counting Heffalumps. And that was worse. Because every Heffalump that he counted was making straight for a pot of Pooh's honey, and eating it all. For some minutes he lay there miserably, but when the five hundred and eighty-seventh Heffalump was licking its jaws, and saying to itself, 'Very good honey this, I don't know when I've tasted better,' Pooh could bear it no longer."[25]

Truth is, stopping doesn't equal recovering.

So what kind of recovery is resilience all about? What qualifies as strategic recovery?

Here's where the research gets interestingly nuanced and helps us become far smarter in our choices. Notice several conclusions from three psychology researchers in Norway, the Netherlands, and the United Kingdom.[26]

One, recovery is a dynamic process and not a static construct.

Effective recovery has to involve both the mind and the body. And furthermore, it means that people have to tailor their recovery strategy to their own individual bodily and mental systems. In other words, one size doesn't fit all. So what types of things do we need to pay attention to?

> People have to tailor their recovery strategy to their own individual bodily and mental systems. In other words, one size doesn't fit all.

Two, tailoring our recovery strategy involves paying attention to our individual circadian rhythms.

We humans have very well-defined internal clocks (circadian rhythms) that regulate several of our biological systems, like temperature, hormones, and the sleep-wakefulness cycle. All of these cycles have direct impact on our energy.

So when it comes to designing our individual work-recovery strategies, we need to pay attention to these rhythms. Though these patterns tend to be common to most people, there is an individualistic design we need to be aware of. These are chronotypes—a specific and unique pattern for each of us.

For example, some of us are more night owls while others of us are more larks (early birds). I'm more of a night owl—which means I tend to have more energy at night than in the morning.

So as we pay attention to the circadian rhythms (our energy cycles during the day and night), we must also be aware that we will most likely lean toward being an owl or a lark. Which means that we will each want to adjust the timing of our high- and low-energy periods to either earlier or later in the day. Experts call this "human energy regulation."[27]

But in spite of this reality, a typical day at work often goes against these natural rhythms, and we wonder why we work so hard with so little result.

"Unfortunately, we often get this wrong. Many employees are flooded with writing and responding to emails throughout their entire morning, which takes them up through lunch [the first energy peak being around 10 a.m. to 12 noon]. They return from lunch having already used up most of their first peak in alertness, and then begin important tasks requiring deep cognitive processing just as they start to move toward the 3pm dip in alertness and energy. We often put employees in a position where they must meet an end-of-workday deadline, so they persist in this important task throughout the 3pm dip. Then, as they are starting to approach the second peak of alertness [from 5 to 6 p.m.], the typical workday ends. For workaholics, they may simply take a dinner break, which occupies some of their peak alertness time, and then work throughout the evening and night as their alertness and cognitive performance decline for the entire duration. And in the worst-case scenario, the employee burns the midnight oil and persists well into the worst circadian dip of the entire cycle, with bleary eyes straining just to stay awake while working on an important task at 3:30am. All of these examples represent common mismatches between an optimal strategy and what people actually do."[28]

In other words, for human regulation to be strategic and effective, we must take into account our natural built-in energy rhythms during day and night. As we plan recovery times, we can be far more aware and conscious of what truly optimizes our lives.

So if, for example, you're more of a lark than an owl, what strategic adjustments would you make to your day's schedule in the previous scenario? If your first energy peak is around 9–10 a.m., would you waste that energy responding to emails or organizing and filing the papers on your desk? Or when you get to work would you dive in on the most important project needing your best attention, the one requiring lots of mental energy and creativity?

Perhaps, then, you would save your routine emails and paperwork to that low-energy phase after lunch and around 3 p.m. And maybe you would wait to have dinner until after 5–6 p.m., since your energy again rises during that phase so you can use it for more of your creative needs.

Maybe you would plan a regular bedtime earlier, rather than later, that gives you eight hours of sleep so you can wake up early in the morning feeling rested.

> Time is a finite resource; energy is a renewable resource. Unlike time, we expend energy, but we can also renew it. We achieve well-being and homeostasis by keeping a dynamic balance between the expenditure and renewal of energy.

You get the idea. Genuine resilience is about making strategic choices—choices that reflect more accurately our individualized human systems and wiring. It's about paying intentional attention to leveraging our biological and emotional systems in ways that optimize our energy and recovery times.

Don't just power through. Think it through. Pay attention. Be smart. And then act accordingly.

4. Achieving Balance is Learning Energy Management

All of human life centers on energy. And here's a secret: time is a finite resource; energy is a renewable resource. Unlike time, we expend energy, but we can also renew it. We achieve well-being and homeostasis by keeping a dynamic balance between the expenditure and renewal of energy.

Here's both the challenging implication and the good news of this reality: you and I have control over this energy dance between output and input. In fact, we have to take responsibility for this process. No one else will do it for us. We are the managers of our energy.

What does this mean? Notice the following perspective and then let me articulate a few implications.

> "'Recovery' is not just the 'absence of demands,' or 'rest.' Such a conceptualization suggests that recovery occurs automatically when demands are (temporarily) removed. And it does not sufficiently acknowledge that recovery should preferably be seen as a dynamic process that aims at restoring the energetic resources. Restoring and expending the energetic resources is a process that takes place continuously throughout the day and is actively controlled or regulated by the individual. 'Recovery' means trying to restore the energy resources, which should generally happen through regulating the state [of our body and our mind]."[29]

First, recovery is not passive; it's active. It's an ongoing process we strategically shape that will result in restoring our systems' energy.

Second, we are responsible for instituting an energy recovery process. Significant others can help support us, like a supervisor offering us time periods to set aside for some recovery or a boss paying attention to the changing energy rhythms during the day and, so far as possible, being allies who ask us to perform tasks that match the rhythms of the day. But for the most part, you and I must take the strategic initiative.

Third, we must know ourselves well enough to shape the most effective recovery experiences at any given time.

If my energy is lagging during the day,

- Do I need a short power nap?
- Do I need a music bath?
- Do I need a brisk walk around the building?
- Do I need a more extended time away from work and responsibilities?
- Do I need to work on some limiting beliefs that are draining energy away from my life, or to change my self-talk in specific ways?
- Do I need a few minutes of guided meditation? Or do I need to sit comfortably in silence?

If I come to the end of a busy work week and my energy feels depleted,

- Do I need a weekend filled with social activities?
- Do I need time for projects around the house?
- Do I need TV relaxation?
- Do I need to sleep more?
- Do I need to read some fun books?
- Do I need to go for a hike in the mountains or a walk along the ocean?

The authors of the above statement refer to restoring energy by means of "regulating the [mind-body] state." In other words, our energy management process must pay attention to our brains and our bodies, determining which of those requires the most current attention.

Fourth, effective recovery takes into account the arousal state.

If I've been particularly physically and mentally active—high arousal because my adrenaline level has been elevated—I need a recovery experience that helps me slow down to let the adrenaline drain away. I need my stress level to drop. The authors refer to this as down-regulating the arousal state.

If, on the other hand, I haven't felt energized or challenged all week, I've felt bored and lackadaisical, not having accomplished anything of significance, I need a recovery time that will pick me up, inspire me, challenge me, and get me active, actually lifting my arousal state. This is called up-regulating.

And lastly, effective recovery involves taking charge of our thoughts and feelings.

Whenever I return home from a speaking engagement in which I've experienced a higher level of arousal and stress, I've learned that I need an intentional recovery experience that involves no other commitments or appointments. I need to simply be home and relax my mind and body. That always recovers my energy. And then I'm ready to re-engage full-heartedly.

But I've discovered that relaxing my mind takes quite a bit of proactive attention. My body may be sitting around doing nothing, but my mind can often scream at me.

The authors talk about recovery involving "overriding thoughts (rumination) and stopping emotions, and regulating attention."

I totally relate to this. I'm the one who has control over this intention (although I will often secure the support of my wife to help me with this process). I have to make the choice to not let myself ruminate and obsess over whatever negative thoughts about my performance might creep into my mind during this time—and trust me, those voices always come to the surface.

"You blew it … If you just hadn't made that one comment … If you would have just been funnier … Nobody was listening … The planners won't give you a good testimonial … Let's face it, you just don't have it as a speaker."

Before I know it, if I allow it, these internal voices have pushed me to the proverbial cliff's edge and I'm about ready to jump to end my career as a public speaker.

I have to choose to not go into debrief and evaluation mode during my recovery time. I wait until my mental energy has increased again. Then I can look more carefully and with far more clarity at how my speaking went. Remember, high adrenaline production always leads to a post-adrenaline depression, or dip in our energy when we find ourselves letting go of everything. Our natural tendency is to begin ruminating about ourselves and our inadequacies, not feeling excited or productive or on top of our game. This is our body's way of getting us to recover and regain energy needed for moving forward when we're ready. So be careful how much you believe your thoughts and feelings during this time. Give yourself permission to recover.

Let's face it. We all have to learn how to regulate our attention and corral our ruminations in order to enjoy energy-recovering resilience.

So here's the summary.

Stopping does not equal recovery. Recovery, to be effective and renewing, has to be strategic. That's why I titled this book "The Strategic Stop." Our human systems are designed to return to equilibrium and balance as long as we're paying attention to what it takes to re-energize them appropriately. This dynamic and individualized process is called rest and resilience.

Contrary to my eighth-grade class' profound motto—"Onward ever, backward never"—the smart way of living life is this: sometimes it's better to take a step back than to keep forging ahead. Sometimes it's smarter to listen to the reverse adage: "Don't just do something, stand there!"

So resist the urge to simply power through. Think it through. Establish some strategic stops for this process. And then act accordingly. This is how you leverage your built-in resilience. And if you do, you will rebuild your energy regularly in ways that increase your attention, productivity, rest, and recovery times. You will live a life more fully alive!

PERSONAL PAUSES

- Based upon this chapter's definition, how do you rate yourself on the resilience scale—with 5 being highly resilient and 1 being extremely low resilience? What specific steps can you take to raise your rating?

- Reshape your daily routines, starting at home and then at work and then back home, according to the timing of your energy cycles throughout the day. Be specific: What times during the day should you do which activities based upon your natural cycles? Be creative and strategic.

- When your energy is lagging during the day, what specific activity(ies) would help re-energize you the most (for example, taking a short walk, listening to music with your headphones, talking to a friend, eating a snack, daydreaming, a short power nap)?

- What are some of the ruminations you find yourself tending to think about after you've gone through a high-energy, high-adrenaline experience? Jot them down. How do you typically deal with those negative or discouraging thoughts and feelings? Can you give yourself permission to simply feel the post-adrenaline depression without having to solve anything or fix your thoughts or pass judgment on yourself?

TEAM PAUSES

⏸ Based upon this chapter's definition, how do you rate yourself on the resilience scale—with 5 being highly resilient and 1 being extremely low resilience? What specific steps can you take to increase that rating? How do you rate your team? What specific steps can you and your team members take to raise the rating?

⏸ Ask your team members what kind of work schedule during the day would most reflect the ebb and flow of their individual energy cycles. In what specific ways could leaders and team members support each other?

⏸ Have an honest conversation with the team about expectations for work outside office hours so everyone has the same general expectations. Articulate specific ways everyone can support each other in minimizing off-hours work.

⏸ Share with each other in a team session: "After a busy week of work, what kind of activity do you most need or want in order to feel fully recovered by the end of the weekend?"

State Your Why

When I was in college, I chose (somewhat naively) to substitute my science class requirement of biology with astronomy. I had no idea what I, a theology major, would encounter in a class full of physics majors. But all I cared about was fueling my passion for and fascination with the night sky and all it contained in the mysteries of the universe.

I had never even taken a high school physics class, much less high-level mathematics. Yet there I was, surrounded by upper-class experts, trying to make heads or tails out of the material. It was brutal. And somewhat embarrassing.

But what kept me from dropping the class, besides my ego, were the evening labs. The professor would often take our class out into the countryside where there were no lights. We would stand in the middle of the cornfields (this was Walla Walla, Washington, after all), gazing up into the clear night sky. The prof would point out and talk about galaxies, constellations, individual stars, and the amazing dynamics of the cosmos visible and invisible to us. It was thrilling to me.

And what I've never forgotten is how to locate the North Star—you know that star, the one that always points the way north? You locate the Big Dipper, run a straight line through the two stars on the right-hand side of the square-like dipper from bottom to top, keep going in that line, and you land on the final star in the handle of the Little Dipper, the brightest one in that grouping of stars. That's the North Star. And without fail, I can still locate it.

Explorers and travelers have navigated by the North Star for millennia with amazing accuracy and effectiveness. It has remained a constant navigational tool in the night sky. Find the star and you can determine your latitude in the Northern Hemisphere with a good degree of accuracy. And when you know your latitude, you can plot your position on a map. You can know where you are. And then you can navigate the path to your destination.

In the world of human development, we use the term *North Star* to refer to those constants in our lives, our sense of purpose and mission and our core values, that direct us back to what is most important to us. We learn to navigate our lives successfully by making sure we are staying focused on our North Star. You can always count on the North Star to remind you where you are and to help you find your way back to where you're going if you've lost your way.

> We learn to navigate our lives successfully by making sure we are staying focused on our North Star.

Here's the way psychologist Dr. Rick Hanson describes the value of knowing your North Star and staying true to it:

"When you find your North Star, you know where you're headed. That alone feels good. Plus, your North Star is (presumably) wholesome and vital, so aiming toward it will bring more and more happiness and benefit to yourself and others. And you can dream bigger dreams and take more chances in life since if you lose your way, you've got a beacon to home in on."[30]

I like what he says about how focusing on and following your North Star gives you the confidence to innovate, take chances, and assume more risks in your life. It's when you're lost without any way of knowing where you are or how to get to where you're wanting to go that you become far more timid. You tend to make safe choices because of the fear of making a bigger mistake or experiencing a terminal failure. You have no beacon to home in on to get you back on track. So you become much more conservative and constricted, rather than expansive and strategic.

"There is a very clear link between courage and the degree of meaning in someone's life; the sense, at a really deep level, that you know why you do things, you know what your life is about. Most fear is fear of the unknown, but when you can answer this root question of what your life is about, that root insecurity is dealt with, and dealing with it makes it so that no fear is as bad as it was before. The more meaning, the more courage, and the less fear."[31]

So the next question is, how do you go about identifying your North Star?

Identifying Your Personal North Star

There's an ancient scripture that says, "Where there is no vision, the people perish." Another translation of this is, "When there is no guidance [vision], people run wild, scattering all over the place with no direction."

Here's the deal: a vision of authentic purpose breathes both life and direction into us. A purpose gives us a powerful, sacred, and holy vehicle to express who we are. Living our purpose enables us to step more fully into our true selves and make the contribution to life that we are uniquely designed for. It focuses our life energies. So let me suggest several steps to identifying your "why" and exploring this purpose in your life. Your goal is to be able to state your purpose in one sentence or two in a way that captivates, inspires, rallies your energy, and truthfully reflects who you are.

First, make a list of all the specific activities and behaviors you've done in the various roles you've had in your lifetime that have brought you positive energy and deep satisfaction. Then identify a common thread or theme between all of those roles.

You've loved doing them. You find yourself doing them in some form or another no matter what setting you're in.

When you have this list, look for common threads between them. What do you notice?

For example, one of my clients really loved public speaking, teaching in the classroom, having one-on-one conversations with people—especially students, coaching soccer, and doing photography. A pretty disparate list. So I probed a bit more.

"What was it about each of those activities that you really enjoyed? Was it just engaging in all of them, or was there something specific in the activities that energized you? Can you think of any common thread between all of them?"

After much reflection and discussion together, he observed, "I think they all involve helping people face obstacles in order to learn to improve and become their best selves."

He loved taking mediocre soccer players and coaching them to excellence. He loved speaking in public about themes and issues to help people expand and develop their lives. He loved mentoring and coaching students about whatever problems they were facing, challenging and prodding them to expand themselves. And though he wasn't the primary photographer on his team, he loved arranging and providing just the right equipment and settings so the photographer could maximize the shots.

It turned out that that phrase or statement really reflected for him what he felt called to be and do in the world. It was his North Star. Describing this with clarity and honesty helped him feel like he was living out his purpose whether he was coaching his soccer team or speaking in public. And this increased vision about his mission and purpose began to empower him to say yes to some things and no to others with equal authority and confidence based upon alignment with his purpose.

Second, take some time to reflect on and answer these questions:
- What are you uniquely designed and prepared to do?
- List the things to which you're consistently drawn. What about them draws you?
- When you were a child, was there something you always wanted to be or do when you grew up?

Look through your answers to these questions. Do you notice any common threads or themes?

The first question calls upon two things—two superpowers—in your life: your unique life experiences, and your unique top strengths.

So make a list of your unique life experiences. Where have you lived, and how has that shaped you? What have you done or experienced that has shaped you and your way of being in the world? For example, sometimes our experiences of brokenness and pain become springboards to a special purpose—those wounds give us a passion and life experience that offers us wisdom to address people in that kind of pain.

Then take Gallup's CliftonStrengths to identify your top five strengths. What do those strengths say about the kind of contribution you are wired to make everywhere you go? Which four strengths categories do your five strengths fall under: Relationship Building, Influencing, Executing, or Strategic Thinking? That will inform you about your strongest areas of contribution and what you are uniquely wired to do and be.

The third question is about identifying your childhood dreams. I encourage you to spend some extra minutes on this question. It's a very intuitive one. Childhood dreams often express a deep, instinctive, innate desire that comes from a pure place. Kids typically haven't been hampered or weighed down yet with all the discrepancies, deliberations, limiting beliefs, image consultants, and ego burdens of adulthood. Their naiveté and innocence often speak truth. So we need to plumb our childhood dreams and desires.

When I was a kid, my dreams were unequivocal. I wanted to be a speaker who traveled the world, experiencing adventures and risky situations and giving talks to people about the meaning of life (whatever that meant to me as a kid). I wanted to be global. I wanted to speak in significant ways. I wanted to be in front of large crowds. And I wanted to help people live a good life in response to what I had to say. I spent hours with this fantasy—dreaming up all kinds of international adventures for myself.

I realize now that that childhood dream was my soul purpose calling out to me about where my strongest place in the world should be. And sure enough, that dream is still alive in me today because it was a piece of my truth. It continues to speak directly to my purpose in life.

Third, try to write down in one sentence what you feel to be your purpose in this world—what are you placed on this planet to do and to contribute?

Remember, this is not about your role(s), the position(s) you hold at work, or the hobbies you engage in. I'll talk about this distinction in the next section.

Purpose is a more expansive, specialized description about the kinds of actions or behaviors you could consider as your mission, whatever role you're in. This is about what excites you and energizes you most in life. This is about what you feel you simply have to be doing while you're alive to feel like your life really counts, about what really matters to you. This is about what kinds of things truly maximize you and express accurately who you are and what it is about you that is unique to you.

Here are some example purpose statements from people I've worked with:

- My purpose is to mentor and coach people to be their best selves.
- My purpose is to create in a way that inspires people with greater possibilities for life.
- My purpose is to be a mirror to help people see the beauty of themselves in a way that gives them more confidence and joy.
- My purpose is to bring compassion and justice into places that need this light.
- My purpose is to fix what is broken and restore it to its original beauty.
- My purpose is to include people who feel left out, giving them a sense of belonging.
- My purpose is to give God-given advantages to the disadvantaged.
- My purpose is to help people find their voice and speak it with confidence and clarity.

So why is all this important? Author Gregg Levoy, in his book *Callings: Finding and Following an Authentic Life*, describes the significance of identifying your purpose this way:

> "That which we cannot name is lost to us, and that which we can name is coaxed into life."[32]

"That which we cannot name is lost to us, and that which we can name is coaxed into life."

When you and I can put words to this sense of purpose, we coax this unique soul-driven expression of self into life with greater power and engagement.

So what is the sentence you've come up with that describes your North Star?

Distinguishing Between Purpose and Role or Job

I spent 25 years as a congregational pastor. So when I transitioned away from that role, in the years that followed, my biggest struggle revolved around this issue: Who am I if I am not a respected pastor of a local congregation within my lifelong denominational system? My identity had been wrapped up in that role my whole life—a role I loved and excelled at and had certainly felt called to.

My challenge was exacerbated by the fact that I had received all my praise and accolades for the high levels of success I had achieved in my life through my role as pastor. Subtly and subconsciously I had made my calling synonymous with my role as a spiritual leader of congregations. So if I was no longer a pastor in that setting, did I not have my calling anymore? Who was I without that role? What was my true identity?

My temptation was to see this loss of role as my biggest challenge moving forward. So the natural instinct was to return somehow to my pastoral role to restore my perceived identity. And realistically, if that were my primary mission, the challenge was indeed a painful and imposing giant because the obstacles to returning to my religious system as a pastor were huge.

As the ensuing months and years went by, I began to come to the realization that equating calling with role is seriously flawed. I started seeing with deepening precision: my roles were actually the delivery systems for and specific expressions of my calling and life purpose. So the reality is that there are multiple roles in life through which I can faithfully and successfully live out my calling. Roles are simply platforms for callings, not the callings themselves.

As I worked through this significant distinction and differentiation, clarity came to me about the true definition of my purpose. My calling wasn't an exclusive proposition: be a pastor or else forsake your calling.

> Roles are simply platforms for callings, not the callings themselves.

Little by little I began to see with more clarity and vision my purpose: I am called to be a guide (a lightbearer) who brings leaders, teams, and groups to the strongest, most authentic expression of themselves—not who I nor anyone else thinks they should be, but who they are perfectly designed to be. My purpose is to be the strategic stop maximizer for leaders, teams, and groups to increase their self-awareness; their relational empathy; and their purpose-driven, innovative collaboration.

I certainly fulfilled that calling in my role as a pastor. But I finally realized that I could fulfill that calling in many different roles even outside the religious system I had grown up in, which now include my current roles as a full-time professional speaker, teacher, author, leadership and team strengths coach, and organizational effectiveness consultant.

My biggest challenge wasn't about how to get back to pastoring in the system I had left. My biggest challenge was about fighting the greatest battle of all, the one we all have to fight: Who am I in a world that demands certain conformity and molding to its image; what is my true, changeless, and absolutely secure identity? And how can I live that out in confident and powerful ways? What is *my* armor, not someone else's? And how can I learn to wear my armor boldly and passionately within the ongoing legend and adventure of my calling, whatever roles I choose to embody and in whatever settings I choose to employ?

I can honestly tell you, this discovery was one of the most liberating, empowering, and confidence-building discoveries of my life. Transitioning away from my church role ended up becoming a profound blessing because it forced me to come to a place of truth and reality—I discovered with greater clarity who I am and what I am truly called to be and do in this world. I caught a powerful glimpse of my North Star. And the exciting thing is that there are no walls or limits to this adventure of purpose and mission for me. My purpose is truly global and so expansive that it will last for my entire lifetime no matter what roles I choose along the way.

So are you clear about your unique purpose in your life? Are you being motivated and driven and empowered by this specific calling? Can you see the differentiation between the roles you're filling right now and your purpose? Keeping your North Star in view is your path to the most fulfilling and meaningful life possible. Losing sight of it means losing one of the most important navigational tools available to you to reaching your best and most purposeful life.

Confronting Your Obstacles

I'll never forget one of our astronomy labs out in the cornfields of Walla Walla, Washington. The professor took us out there to escape the brighter lights of the town. The views of the cosmos were stellar in pitch-black darkness. He told us that it typically takes 20 minutes for the eyes to get used to the dark so they can see clearly. "So whenever a car drives by," he cautioned us, "be sure to cover up your eyes until the car passes by. That way you'll escape having to wait so long to see the night sky again."

Sure enough. It worked like a charm.

Until this one time. An oncoming car didn't drive by; it stopped off the road right in front of us. Like obedient students, we all kept our hands covering our eyes. We heard the car door slam shut, footsteps approaching, and then a rather authoritative voice say, "Excuse me, folks. What are you doing out here in the cornfields this time of night?"

The professor apparently walked up to him. I say "apparently" because we all were still covering our eyes with our hands. The prof said, "So sorry, Officer. We are an astronomy class, and this is our evening lab. We're here away from the city lights so we can look at the night sky without distraction. I've told the students to cover their eyes every time a car drives by so their eyes stay tuned to the darkness."

The officer wasn't convinced. "I've had some complaints from passersby that there is a drug party going on out here. All they saw as they drove by were these young people hiding their faces. You sure there aren't any drugs here?" he challenged.

The prof continued to prove his point. Finally, the officer seemed to understand what was going on. When he got into his squad car and drove off, we all busted out laughing. The only thing that could have made this experience more memorable would have been for the university to have had to bail us all out of jail. Tuition credit.

Here's the reality: all of us face obstacles to seeing our North Star, which in turn can potentially derail us from living out our purpose. Notice some of these obstacles.

Distractions

For meaningful stargazing, city lights are a major distraction. They compete for our eyes' attention and focus. What does this distraction look like in your life?

I coached and consulted with a large congregation that had a massive number of programs and activities going on all the time. These events were quite impressive, actually. This was a congregation involved in lots of great things.

What I noticed, however, was a lack of common purpose among all the activities. There was no unifying theme. People were busy leading or participating. But a clear sense of mission was missing. Busyness, even with good things and good intentions, was distracting from a clear vision of what their overarching purpose and mission were. The North Star was missing.

As a result, the leaders and other participants were feeling tired, exhausted, and burned out. The congregants were feeling frazzled with so many activities to attend. This was not a sustainable or strategic energy management approach.

So I worked with the leaders to begin a process of strategic visioning—elevating the value of taking regular strategic stops. What is this congregation's primary purpose and mission—what is the North Star by which everything is evaluated to determine whether or not they are moving in the right direction? The goal isn't simply to be busy doing good things. The goal is to be faithful to a strategic direction that comes from a clear vision of calling and purpose. It's about choosing to fulfill its God-given mission by means of its God-given, unique design. And everyone in that congregation needs to know what this is and then see it in action.

Once this clarity was developed, energy began to rise. Why? Because a number of activities were discontinued when it became apparent that, though they were good things, they weren't in alignment with the congregation's North Star. They were distractions. And the busyness that came with the activities was draining vital energy.

> The goal isn't simply to be busy doing good things. The goal is to be faithful to a strategic direction that comes from a clear vision of calling and purpose.

This is one of the easiest distractions to get caught up in personally as well as organizationally. We become blinded by the bright lights of the next shiny object. We're jumping from one initiative or idea to another simply because it looks interesting, exciting, cutting-edge, or innovative. We confuse busyness or even innovation with strategic vision.

The result of looking into all these headlights is that we lose our ability to see the North Star clearly and compellingly. Like our prof told our astronomy class, we have to put our hands over our eyes temporarily in order to get accustomed to see the star well enough to follow it.

Let's not confuse busyness and activity with purpose-driven momentum. Strategic stops are a necessary way to keep this distinction in view. We need times to put our hands over our eyes to keep us from being distracted so we can see our North Star and establish effective ways to follow it.

Detractors

I saw this meme in my Twitter feed: "Don't let someone dim your light simply because it's shining in their eyes."

Almost without fail, when we get clear on our North Star and follow its light with boldness and confidence, there are people who will become detractors and obstacles to us on our way forward.

Like the police officer that night when my astronomy class was in the cornfields, detractors will question our right to be where we are or to go where we're going or to be who we're becoming or to follow our convictions. Like those drive-by lookers who reported our class as druggies dancing in the fields, detractors will judge us, criticize us, and even spread rumors about us. They are threatened by our sense of freedom, confidence, and direction. They will disagree with our North Star, accusing us of being on the wrong path or of shining our light too brightly.

> "Don't let someone dim your light simply because it's shining in their eyes."

When you know your mission, your unique purpose, you will face resistance—internal and external.

Dr. Randy Pausch, author of the New York Times bestseller *The Last Lecture*, as he faced terminal pancreatic cancer at age 47, wrote:

"The brick walls are there for a reason. The brick walls are not there to keep us out. The brick walls are there to give us a chance to show how badly we want something. Because the brick walls are there to stop the people who don't want it badly enough. They're there to stop the other people."[33]

A brick wall is a powerful metaphor to describe your detractors. They are tests of your true will, passion, and conviction. How important is following your North Star? Are you willing to follow at all costs? Is your purpose so compelling that you will stay true to it no matter what people say to you or about you? North Star trumps brick wall every time.

One of my clients ran into his brick wall. It was his dad. His father had always wanted him to be a physician like himself. So my client complied. But as the years went by, it became clear to him that this path wasn't really his passion—his sense of calling and purpose were quite different. And as he made this discovery, he told me he wasn't sure how to navigate this change with his father. He was certain his dad would be very upset with him.

But brick walls exist in order to show us how badly we want to move toward our North Star.

So with some fear and trepidation, my client went home and had the brave and strategic conversation with his father. Sure enough, his dad was upset—disappointed—and expressed fear that if his son changed careers he wouldn't be able to sustain his way of life. Turns out the father was simply wanting his son to have a lifestyle for him and his family that the father's current career was providing him. Dad was afraid that if his son moved away from his current career his lifestyle would become financially unsustainable.

My client's courageous pushback with his father created a turning point in their relationship—in this case, for the better. His father could clearly see that his son's desire for change wasn't some whim or midlife crisis. It had been well thought-out and strategically considered and planned. His father realized how proud he was of his son's intent and passion. And both of them developed a new respect for each other.

Rather than simply judging our detractors—those brick walls—it's more effective to use them as learning tools.

A good coaching friend of mine likes to say, "There are no problems to be solved—just more truth to be revealed. All problems are a gateway into a deeper truth that is longing to emerge."

Rather than dismissing these people as simply being problems, take a strategic stop. Ask yourself strategic questions that can lead to greater transformation:

- What does this obstacle tell me about how clear or how important my purpose is to me?
- What can I learn more about myself, about this situation, about the person or people involved?
- Why is their behavior or this task pushing my buttons?
- What is it about my thinking and attitude that causes me such pain?
- Are there any changes I need to make in how I'm showing up?
- Do I need to adjust my attitude toward the other person or people?
- Do I have any responsibility in this situation or outcome? If so, can I acknowledge it and learn from it? If not, can I learn the art of letting things go?
- Can I step into forgiveness or compassion more honestly while still holding people accountable for their behavior?

Obstacles can be vehicles of deeper truth, personal growth, and relational connection. So don't dismiss them too quickly.

Lean into them and listen to what they're saying to you. Use them as vehicles to follow your North Star, letting their opposition remind you of how important your North Star is to you. Your North Star lights the way to the path that brings you the most meaning, fulfillment, and adventure throughout your lifetime.

> Obstacles can be vehicles of deeper truth, personal growth, and relational connection. So don't dismiss them too quickly.

PERSONAL PAUSES

⏸ Make a list of all the specific activities and behaviors you've done in the various roles you've had in your lifetime that brought you positive energy and deep satisfaction. Then identify a common thread/theme between all of those roles.

⏸ Take some time to answer these questions: 1. What are you uniquely designed and prepared to do (like your life experience and your strengths)? 2. List the things to which you're consistently drawn. What about them draws you? Do you enjoy engaging in them and why? 3. When you were a child, was there something you always wanted to be or do when you grew up? 4. Look through your answers to these questions. Do you notice any common threads or themes among them? What are they?

⏸ Now try to write down in one sentence what you feel to be your purpose—what are you placed on this planet to do and to contribute that is uniquely you? What does reading this statement feel like to you—does it resonate, give you positive energy, feel true to you?

⏸ Who is a person that tends to be the biggest detractor for you living your purpose? How are you dealing with that person? Is that working? What could you do differently to not let them sidetrack you from what is most important?

TEAM PAUSES

⏸ Have everyone on the team share a description of what they feel is their strongest, most valuable contribution to the team. "What do you simply love doing the most and why?"

⏸ Sharing question: "Identify the biggest distraction that keeps you from living out your sense of purpose. What is one thing you can do to manage this distraction?"

⏸ "Don't let someone dim your light simply because it's shining in their eyes." Sharing question: "Share a time when you experienced someone else trying to dim your light—saying you were too much, or too bright, or too something. How did it feel? How did you respond?"

⏸ Come up with a team purpose statement. "Our purpose as a team is to ..." Another way to look at this is, what makes your team unique from other teams? What is your competitive advantage as a team that sets you apart from other teams? Could it be your strengths combination? Your unique contribution to the organization? What is your team's North Star?

Strengthen Self-Awareness

What do the most successful, high-performing people have in common?

This was the question authors and researchers Camille Sweeney and Josh Gosfield asked very successful people in numerous industries like food, business, sports, music, entertainment, and the arts. They assumed that the answers would be talent, persistence, dedication, and luck. What they discovered, however, was completely surprising.

The key common ingredient with high-performing, successful people was self-reflection. Self-awareness. They described this as the ability and choice to engage in "rigorous self-evaluation."[34]

For example, they highlighted the story of Martina Navratilova, now known as the greatest female tennis player of her era in the world.

In 1981, she lost a championship match to Chris Evert. She was stunned. Devastated. But rather than wallow in her disappointment, she focused on questioning her assumptions about being able to rely on her instincts and natural talent alone. She courageously launched herself into a rigorous self-evaluation process.

Hiring new coaches, she began to look carefully at every aspect of her tennis game: her grip on the racket, her swing, her physiology and conditioning, her mental attitude, the speed and strength of her arms and legs. From top to bottom, she re-evaluated. She deconstructed and then reconstructed her entire game.

When she finally re-emerged into the circuit, and then ultimately played another big match against Chris Evert, she won. And then kept winning. And developed the enviable reputation of being the greatest female tennis player in the world.

We live at a time in history in which we are literally bombarded with information of all kinds on a daily basis. Everyone and everything are competing for our attention. And now, with smartphones, we are never away from this assault. Consequently, we experience a kind of mental overload, overstimulation, and exhaustion.

The need for developing the art of quiet and honest self-reflection is greater now than ever. A detox of the mind. Stepping back to see through the information smog to discern what is truly important, to gain deeper awareness about ourselves, and to understand who we truly are in the midst of all this commotion so we can be grounded and centered in our individual and authentic identity. That is where our greatest personal power resides.

As Martina Navratilova showed, self-reflection is not for the faint of heart. It isn't a lackadaisical; que será, será; take-it-as-it-comes; hope-it-happens process, either. It's rigorous, it's regular, and it's strategic. But it pays rich dividends. Just look at the most successful people and notice the impressive resilience they have and what it has empowered them to accomplish in the world.

So how do we do this effectively? Let me suggest three parts to the process of self-reflection. The first two will be this chapter; the third in the next chapter.

1. Shaping the Space for Self-Reflection

We begin by being intentional about setting aside regular times and spaces for reflection. I call these strategic stops.

The story is told of one of the 4th century Desert Fathers of early Christianity:

"He travelled once on pilgrimage to Rome. Here he was told of a celebrated recluse, a woman who lived always in one room, never going out. Skeptical about her way of life—for he was himself a great wanderer—he called on her and asked: 'Why are you sitting here?' To this she replied: 'I am not sitting. I am on a journey.'"[35]

She may have been physically sitting on a chair, but for her, that space in time involved being on a journey—her own strategic stop—an inward journey of reflection, prayer, and deeper connection with herself and with her God. The chair simply represented the physical space where she carved out time for her journey of reflection.

The perpetual wanderer couldn't understand her choice or way of being. He was used to always going, always moving to the next adventure or pilgrimage to the next holy site. His was a life of constant motion without any strategic stops along the way. He was always going somewhere else to find the divine, missing it in the present moment.

This is one of our contemporary dangers, too. We are so busy paying attention to all the urgent things demanding time and energy—work projects, family needs, children's activities, house and yard work, social commitments, church or civic engagements. Our calendars are packed full with appointments: doctors, dentists, music lessons, potlucks, concerts, sporting events, meetings, emails, travel time … And it never ends. We can never catch up and breathe a sigh of relief that we're finally done with it all and can take a well-deserved break.

The tragedy is that we have consigned ourselves to living very superficial lives. Not that these activities are shallow. But we find ourselves without time and energy to go deeper with ourselves, much less with others. We're perpetual wanderers instead of sitters.

I find it significant that Jesus—a truly self-actualized being—who was continually surrounded by people and their demands was so busy that his friends and family thought he would go mad. So for his sake (they assured themselves) they rebuked him for working so hard and letting himself be drawn to so many needy people all the time.

And yet, in a life of such busyness doing the important work of loving, caring, and healing people, Jesus insisted on staying true to his personal strategy. He refused to bypass one of his most prioritized practices—every night, he would spend time alone, away from the hustle and bustle of the crowds and even his closest friends, to give undivided attention to his own soul and heart, to remembering and staying focused on his true identity, and to connecting with his God.

> The tragedy is that we have consigned ourselves to living very superficial lives. Not that these activities are shallow. But we find ourselves without time and energy to go deeper with ourselves, much less with others. We're perpetual wanderers instead of sitters.

Jesus shaped space for self-care, self-renewal, and self-reflection. And he stuck to this strategic commitment no matter how hectic life got. Is it any wonder he was so self-actualized?

Let me give some contemporary examples. Some of the most successful people in today's world have seen the value of reclaiming the art of self-reflection in their lives. They intentionally carve out time for this kind of thinking. And notice the variety of ways they engage in strategic stops for self-reflection. This practice can look different for all of us.

Bill Gates (founder of Microsoft and now leading a multi-billion-dollar nonprofit foundation), Mark Zuckerberg (CEO of Facebook), and Warren Buffet (one of the most successful investors of all time) "read extensively, safeguard time for personal development projects, and constantly seek new stimulus and perspectives."[36]

"Jeff Weiner, CEO at LinkedIn, blocks between 90 minutes and two hours every day for reflection and describes those buffers as 'the single most important productivity tool' he uses.

"Susan Hakkarainen, Chairman and co-CEO of Lutron told us, 'I use 40-minute walks to reflect and I read articles for personal stimulus and development over my morning coffee.'

"Yana Kakar, Global Managing Partner of Dalberg, reserves 3 two-hour blocks of time for reflection each week. She comments, 'Thinking is the one thing you can't outsource as a leader. Holding this time sacred in my schedule despite the deluge of calls, meetings, and emails is essential.'

"Others concentrate reflection in a single day. Brian Scudamore, the serial entrepreneur at O2E Brands, sets aside all of Monday for thinking and organizing the rest of the week, which is filled with back-to-back meetings. He also creates a suitable environment for deep thinking by not going into the office on Monday.

"Phil Libin, former Evernote CEO, uses time in airplanes to disconnect from daily work."[37]

These hugely busy people have committed themselves to initiating regular strategic stops for the purpose of self-reflection, self-improvement, and personal growth and development.

Why do they prioritize this? After all, they have so much bombarding them every minute of the day. How can they possibly take time for something else?

Did you notice Yana Kakar's motivation?

"Holding this time sacred in my schedule ... is essential."

She calls this priority, this space in time that she's chosen to set aside, sacred. Essential.

By using the word *sacred*, she's saying that the value of this practice outweighs any time challenges. And the value comes from how she sees it: holy, essential to her most fundamental human nature and who she is as a human being. She sees this time as a tool to assist her in staying true to herself and her identity and achieving her fullest potential. In the midst of all the voices in her world that are clamoring for her attention—voices that are saying, "Be this! Do this! Be more of this! Do more of that! Think like this! Side with us instead of them! Deserve our approval!"—she realizes that in order to not lose herself along the way, to not lose her own voice, to stay true to herself and continue being her true self, she must prioritize her time by maintaining her strategic stop, which sustains her identity and keeps her centered and grounded in her truth.

What empowers her to prioritize it? She has identified her strongest motivation—sacred. This isn't in a religious sense. It's in a value, priority sense. Without this kind of specified motivation she has attached to her practice, it would be too easy to allow the practice to go by the wayside whenever something urgent invades her time.

This is a powerful strategy that empowers prioritization: label the practice—choose a word (like *sacred*—or synonyms like *blessed, hallowed, revered, consecrated,* or *can't-do-without*) that signifies high value to you to help you remember its significance and your commitment to it.

And then as often as possible, keep the practice to a specified time of the day or week. That's how it gets embedded within the culture of your whole life. And you'll find yourself looking forward to and anticipating that time when you meet yourself with a loving embrace, knowing that you are becoming more fully whole and more fully you.

Putting Self-Reflection Into Practice

So what could shaping this kind of a strategic stop, an intentional and regular space for self-reflection, look like in your life? Here are some follow-up questions you can add that might help you identify the why, how, and where.

1. **Identifying Blocks.** What conflicting feelings or thoughts are you having right now as you read this? Resonance? Resistance? Are they reasons why prioritizing this kind of strategic stop won't work in your life? After all, you're faced with some unique challenges to your time management:

- "I've got kids to pay attention to all day long. I can't find any alone time for this kind of luxury. Self-reflection? I can barely survive having to think about my family and managing the entire household, let alone think about myself. Jesus didn't have any children to worry about. Those CEOs can use their work time for this practice. And CEOs probably can afford to have nannies taking care of their children. My life is just too filled up and structured for this!"
- "I take care of my aging parents who live with us. That's almost a full-time job in addition to my actual full-time work. Alone time for self-reflection is an impossibility."
- "Self-reflection is selfish. Too much navel-gazing. A good life is about thinking more of others than of yourself. Didn't Jesus talk about denying yourself?"
- "Self-reflection is a waste of time. Life is about doing your best with whatever you have. Working hard. Caring for your family. Being honest. Having integrity. If you do those things, you're living a good life."
- "Even if I had the time to set aside, I don't have any clue about what I would do during it. What does 'self-reflection' even mean? I'm not a very reflective person. I'm more action-oriented."

These are all reasons I've heard through the years from people who don't think self-reflection is important or feel like they're just too busy for it. I'll be dealing with these concerns in the next two sections. But it's important to first be able to personally identify our mental and emotional blocks for engaging in this practice. And as you think about them, label them as either reasons or excuses.

2. Identifying Schedule. Once you've identified the blocks keeping you from setting aside time for self-reflection, decide in what part of your daily or weekly schedule this strategic stop would best fit.

- How much time in each sitting can you devote to this practice? Can you establish several slots of time during the week? How much time in a slot?
- Can you utilize an activity that you already do regularly and include some self-reflection? Like lunchtime at work or a work break? One of your walking or running times? Or your commute time?

3. Identifying Location. Is there a suitable environment that you would find especially energizing and conducive for this strategic stop?

- At home? Do you have a favorite chair? A study? Your bedroom? Out on the deck or patio? A swing in the back yard? In a park near your house?
- At work? At your desk? A meeting room or phone room you can use for a few minutes? A cafeteria? A break room?
- Traveling or commuting? In the car, airplane, or public transportation? Do you have noise-canceling headphones or earbuds?
- A favorite outdoor spot, like a nature walk through the forest or on the beach? A green space near your home?

These are just some of the questions to ask in establishing your own parameters for how and where you can engage in a strategic stop for self-reflection. Add to these lists as you think about it so that you can make it your own and come up with what works for you.

The significant issue here is to make a commitment to carve out some times. And then just do it. Experiment with it. Be creative. Nothing you start is put into concrete. Allow yourself flexibility—you can make changes along the way. Try different approaches. Try various locations. Feel it out and see what works for you.

Then resolve to build consistency into this practice. This is what will begin to embed self-reflection into the rhythm of your life and personal culture. Keep showing up.

And finally, remember your motivation—that word you've chosen to label the reason for your regular practice. State it often to yourself. Like Yana Kakar's mantra: "Holding this time sacred in my schedule ... is essential." This strategic stop is consecrated time for you. Remind yourself often.

> This strategic stop is consecrated time for you. Remind yourself often.

Now let's reflect on part two of the self-reflection process—what to do during these strategic stops.

2. Utilizing the Process of Self-Awareness

My wife and I were car shopping three years ago. It was definitely time to replace my 1999 Nissan Altima that had almost 150,000 miles on it.

So we put together a list of wants for the car. What features were absolutely important to us to have? We concluded that we were willing to buy a used vehicle, but one that was only a couple of years old. We wanted it to be a Honda Accord sedan EX, V6, with a black exterior and leather interior, and—without question—it must have a navigation system. We refused to look at any car that didn't have a nav system.

You can imagine our excitement when we finally located the car that matched our entire list of requirements. Driving it off the lot was an amazing moment of joy for me! My dream come true!

But something interesting happened not long after that ecstatic beginning. We found ourselves using the navigation unit less and less. The very accessory we refused to look at any car without. Not that we didn't need it. But our iPhones were much easier to use and, eventually, they were more effective. We ended up using their built-in GPS way more often—while walking, driving, and essentially anytime we needed to check traffic or travel times before our trips. We carried our phones with us everywhere we went. Handy. Always accessible. Light.

One of the reasons we no longer used the car navigation system was because it was never updated. It's still operating with 2014 software. So as the years have gone by, its travel information has become more and more obsolete. Whereas our iPhone GPS apps get updated regularly. And they have more useful features for knowing where we, where we're going, and the best way to get there.

I've met a number of people through the years who are operating on very outdated personal GPS systems. Their awareness of themselves and, correspondingly, of others in their lives is extremely low. It's like they're walking around lost and don't know how to find their way. So they're simply stumbling and bumbling around, running into people along the way.

Which means that their ability to regulate themselves appropriately in life settings is underdeveloped. For example, they are compelled to talk way more than they listen; they don't understand their feelings and how to deal with them in healthy ways; they stick their feet in their mouths more often than not; they don't know how to empathize with others; their self-esteem is low, so with a lack of confidence they either withdraw or become aggressive; they feel threatened by others, so they demean or diminish them; they feel incapable of affirming and loving people, mostly because often they don't affirm or love themselves in healthy ways.

The list of these personal and relational deficits is almost endless.

Have you met people like this?

My wife and I were attending a national conference for the speaking association we belong to. It's always a delightful time to learn more about the skills and business of public speaking as well as meet all kinds of professionals in our industry.

I always enjoy connecting with new people and finding out about their lives, what they're doing, how they feel about it, and what makes them really passionate and energized in their work.

One gentleman we met began talking about his work. And soon he was talking about his life. And he made sure we knew all about his many impressive accomplishments. He was dropping names left and right of famous people he knew. He kept talking. And talking.

My wife and I could hardly get a word in edgewise. Though we tried at times to interject information about what we do and what we speak about, he never stopped long enough to listen to us. He hardly asked any questions about our lives. And the one or two questions he did ask us, we had no more gotten out two sentences when he jumped back in and turned the conversation back on himself. And off he went. Again.

He was so obtuse and unaware, that as my wife and I finally extricated ourselves from his presence, we looked at each other, shook our heads in amazement, and broke out laughing. His lack of self-awareness was so blatant that it moved past sad to angering to absurd.

Here's the tragedy. This man was very smart and successful to a degree, but he was completely clueless about how he was coming across. He didn't realize this was happening and that he could actually fix it for his benefit and the benefit of others.

> Every person has a built-in GPS system to help navigate their journey through life as effectively as possible. We are wired with the capacity to understand ourselves and others and to use that information to effectively regulate ourselves and our responses to others.

Every person has a built-in GPS system to help navigate their journey through life as effectively as possible. We are wired with the capacity to understand ourselves and others and to use that information to effectively regulate ourselves and our responses to others.

But judging by how so many people actually present themselves in life, it's clear their current software is outdated. They've never made use of the new updates along the way. So they get lost ... and often don't even know it. Then they blame the consequences on everyone else but themselves.

Sound like anybody you know?

Leveraging Our Pathways to Change

There is a lot of talk these days about emotional intelligence, often abbreviated as EQ (emotional quotient). EQ is fundamental to our capacity as human beings to succeed in life. EQ determines how we think, feel, and behave in all situations with ourselves and with others.

IQ (intelligence quotient) is our cognitive capacity. It is our ability to learn, to process information. According to most experts, throughout a person's lifetime IQ can only be increased by a few percentage points. It is essentially a fixed or stable setting.

EQ, however, is flexible. It can be increased substantially through a person's lifetime through learning and practice. EQ is core to our internal GPS software system.

Why is this important? Because research reveals that EQ, not IQ, is the foundation for effective performance and success in life.

Here's the way authors Travis Bradbury and Jean Greaves put in their best-selling book *Emotional Intelligence 2.0*: "EQ is so critical to success that it accounts for 58 percent of performance in all types of jobs. It is the single biggest predictor of performance in the workplace and the strongest driver of leadership and personal excellence."[38]

The good news is, you and I can do something about our EQ. We can update our inner GPS software. And when we do, our navigation through life becomes far more effective.

Central to this process of software update is plasticity, the term neurologists use to describe the brain's ability to change and transform by building new connections (neural networks).[39] These new connections essentially "speed the efficiency of thought."[40] This is what makes possible new ways of thinking that, in turn, produce new ways of behaving.

In other words, when we identify a change we want to produce in how we act or react to whatever might be a trigger for us, the more we practice the new thought or behavior, the more connections are being created in our brains, and the stronger those new pathways become. Until finally, with lots of practice, a new habit is formed.

So this is the marvelous and wonderful human design you and I can leverage to increase our emotional intelligence. We have within our grasp the ability to bring powerful and transformational change into our lives.

Self-Awareness is Critical to Emotional Intelligence
So we have the brain wiring to change. Great news!

The problem is that many of us don't realize that we need to change. We're simply not self-aware enough to know. We're not paying attention to how we're coming across to others. We're not noticing the cues that are signaling people's responses to us. We're not aware of why we're reacting so negatively or what we're actually feeling inside that is producing our negative behavior. Or we're choosing to ignore all of these signs along the way.

One of the four crucial software pieces to our EQ GPS system is self-awareness. Without it, growth that is critical to personal and relational health simply doesn't happen.

"Self-awareness is a foundational skill; when you have it, self-awareness makes the other emotional intelligence skills much easier to us. As self-awareness increases, people's satisfaction with life—defined as their ability to reach their goals at work and at home—skyrockets. Self-awareness is so important for job performance that 83 percent of people high in self-awareness are top performers, and just 2 percent of bottom performers are high in self-awareness. Why is this so? When you are self-aware you are far more likely to pursue the right opportunities, put your strengths to work and—perhaps most importantly—keep your emotions from holding you back."[41]

Here's a self-reflection question: When was the last time you spent some moments thinking about why you blew up in a given situation—whether you had a big external outburst of anger or whether you simply felt angry inside and let it stew for a long time?

Many of our arguments and fights in our relationships, for example, center on triggers that set off deep feelings inside of us. Here is where self-awareness is so vital.

First of all, do we know what is triggering us in those moments? Is it something the person said to us? How they said it? Something we thought they were implying about us? Is it totally unrelated to that person but reminding us of another event with someone different?

Second, do we know what feelings inside us are being triggered? Is it anger, sadness, a sense of inadequacy, resentment, jealousy, powerlessness, fear? Is there a limiting belief that is being triggered—like, "I'm not good enough," or "I have no power on my own"? Or "I'm a victim in this situation with no control over the outcome"?

And third, have we developed the capacity to manage those feelings in healthy ways that are not destructive to ourselves or to the one we're fighting with, and instead ultimately lead to building deeper connections with that person? Do we know what to do with those deep feelings? Do we stuff them ("It's better to simply not think about it," or "I'm afraid if I talk about it will hurt me or hurt them")? Do we talk about it honestly then or at a later time?

You can see that without self-awareness, we give ourselves no opportunity to learn about ourselves and we give our situations no possibility to be positively transformed. The result is that we give up our agency to the situation or circumstance. It controls us rather than us controlling it.

Self-awareness isn't just about looking at our inadequacies, weaknesses, and inabilities. It's also about knowing what energizes us, what makes us feel strong and powerful, what we're really good at, and why we have certain tendencies to do things that bring positive feelings and outcomes.

This kind of self-awareness increases what I call conscious competence. The more we're aware of why we're strong at something (the conscious part), the more we can step into those behaviors and maximize our competence. Accurate self-awareness gives us this higher performance capacity.

But even self-awareness of positive qualities like strengths is threatening to some people.

In the strengths coaching I do with leaders and teams—in which we're focusing on our brains' natural preferences, things we tend to do instinctively that really energize us—when I ask people to debrief what it felt like to share their strengths out loud with two other people, many state that they felt uncomfortable. Even more uncomfortable than when I ask them to share about some of the shadow sides to their strengths.

When I ask them why it's so uncomfortable, they say that people aren't used to being open about where they shine. We're taught not to brag or puff ourselves up in front of others. We're supposed to be humble and think of others before we think of ourselves. We don't want to be seen as arrogant, proud, or better than others.

So the challenge is that many of us aren't comfortable talking or thinking about our feelings—good or bad—or our behaviors—strong or weak, healthy or unhealthy. And we end up allowing discomfort (which is itself a feeling, ironically enough) to keep us from self-awareness. "It's just better to not talk about these things," many people have said to me.

But without self-awareness we cannot experience a growing EQ. We are choosing to go through life without the necessary software updates for our internal GPS systems. And then every once in a while, when things go bad, when relationships crumble, when our jobs suffer, when we're feeling bad inside more often than not, we aren't able to navigate successfully our way through to contentment, joy, and success.

> Without self-awareness we cannot experience a growing EQ. We are choosing to go through life without the necessary software updates for our internal GPS systems.

This is why the leaders in the last section, along with so many successful people like them, prioritize strategic stops—deliberate and intentional pauses for self-reflection and increased self-awareness. They realize the powerful value of setting aside these sacred moments. And they acknowledge that they cannot live well without them.

Utilizing Slow Thinking vs. Fast Thinking to Increase Self-Awareness

There are two kinds of thinking that we call upon throughout the day. Brain science refers to slow thinking and fast thinking. Slow thinking is essentially more reflective. This is when a person stops to take time to examine "underlying assumptions, core beliefs, and knowledge, while drawing connections between apparently disparate pieces of information."[42]

Fast thinking is more reactive, like when you're riding a bicycle or driving a car or playing Whack-a-Mole at the county fair. You don't have a lot of time to spend in reflection. You're having to make quick decisions, going on instinct or habit.

Each kind of thinking uses a different part of the brain. Daniel Kahneman, in his book *Thinking, Fast and Slow*, points out that slow thinking is negatively correlated to fast thinking. "Reflective thinking (slow and deliberative) and reactive thinking (fast and instinctual) effectively exist at opposite ends of a switch. When one is 'on,' the other is 'off.'"[43]

So you can see our challenge. In today's fast-paced culture, we're constantly having to make quick decisions and choices while being bombarded with a deluge of variety, information, and needs clamoring for our immediate attention. We're having to tap into fast thinking all the time. And when the switch for that part of our brain is on, the other is off.

No wonder it's so difficult to slow down for self-reflection and self-awareness. It takes intentionality to flip the switch in our brains. It takes a deliberate choice to engage in slow thinking in order to examine ourselves, our biases, our choices—to evaluate our thought patterns, triggers, and typical responses to internal and external environments.

You and I simply cannot increase our emotional intelligence unless we make the choice to create the necessary space to flip the brain switch and engage in this kind of self-reflection.

As I went home after an important managers team session in a company I was coaching, I found myself thinking back on the session as I often do, reflecting on what went well and what could have been improved. But this time I began fixating on a couple of interactions with two of the leaders. Those interactions had obviously triggered something in me because I was starting to judge myself very harshly. It wasn't long before I was catastrophizing and globalizing.

"I really blew it! I'm a terrible coach! They might never invite me back! I'm through!"

Now you see what I mean by catastrophizing and globalizing. These are two telltale signs of taking an internal trigger and, when feeling discouraged, putting your own interpretation on events. And wow, was I ever.

If I would have left it at that, I would have lost a golden opportunity for significant personal growth. Not to mention that I could've then spiraled completely down and, turning a mole hill into Mt. Everest, had a difficult time recovering.

Though I spent a rather fitful night dreaming about my limiting beliefs, the next morning I chose to step into my wife's and my weekly ritual—one of our strategic stops—Saturday breakfast at our favorite café punctuated by our sharing question: What is a high and low of this last week?

This weekly sacred space gave me opportunity to reflect on why I was feeling so emotionally triggered. And with the help of my wife's compassionate listening ear and wise feedback, I was able to look at myself transparently and honestly and ask the strategic and rigorous self-evaluation questions. Then I could identify some transformative learnings.

The next level of self-awareness is to be able to do this thinking right on the spot—identifying what you're feeling and bringing yourself back to a place of contentment and joy. I find myself being able to do this easily in some situations and not as well in others. In this particular case, I realized later that the stakes felt a lot higher to me than normal because of the people in the group session. I was feeling more pressure internally, which knocked me off my centering-space enough to keep me from realizing in the moment what was happening and how to immediately manage it.

I can truthfully say that the weekly strategic stop my wife and I had that day after was a game-changer for me. It helped me come face to face with who I am, what's true about me, and how my sensitive parts can actually be used to help shape me into a more effective leader.

And most encouragingly, rather than wanting to continue spiraling down the rabbit hole of extinction, I felt empowered and excited to jump back into the fray, doing what I love doing most and what I do so well—maximizing leaders and teams—and doing it with renewed self-awareness, self-clarity, and self-confidence.

I flipped the switch. And it was totally worth it.

Reaping the Benefits

I grew up in a religious tribe that taught the value of tithing. It was typically applied to finances. We took one tenth of our monthly income and returned it. This practice was a reminder that everything belongs to God and has been given to us by God, so in an act of trusting gratitude we gave it back to God every month for the support of the ministries and services of the church locally and globally.

I still practice tithing to the causes of nonprofits I believe in because it's an act of trust in the belief in the power of gratitude, generosity, and compassion. It's an act of trust that what we unselfishly put out into the world comes back to us. I've discovered that living in trust and gratitude increases the health of our body's biological, psychological, relational, and spiritual systems.

That's with money. But have you ever considered tithing your time? Interestingly, AOL CEO Tim Armstrong has instructed his executives to spend one tenth of each working week in reflective thinking and self-reflection.

I'm inspired by this vision. Imagine it. Devoting this kind of intentional time—what I call a strategic stop—every week for the purpose of thinking, reflecting, growing, developing, improving, and being grateful. Tithing your time.

Imagine working for an organization whose executives are engaging in the practice of this kind of strategic stop. Leaders typically set the tone and the culture. In this case, having leaders modeling this intention and priority has the potential of elevating the importance of a culture based upon personal growth, development, and creative thinking.

Here's the way former CEO and author Dan Ciampa describes the importance of this value:

"The French philosopher Blaise Pascal pointed out that 'All of humanity's problems come from man's inability to sit quietly in a room alone.' He didn't mean sitting quietly in front of a laptop responding to emails. The best thinking comes from structured reflection ... There's strong evidence that replaying events in our brain is essential to learning. While the brain records and holds what takes place in the moment, the learning from what one has gone through—that is, determining what is important and what lessons should be learned—happens after the fact during periods of quiet reflection."[44]

Leaders, teams, and entire organizations cannot afford, in this fast-paced, competitive, and ever-changing world, to neglect creative thinking and innovation. And the regular practice that supports this environment is the strategic stop—carving out intentional times for reflection and evaluation, thinking, and learning.

In fact, one CEO and author has called this ability to focus "a competitive advantage in the world today."[45]

Tithing your time is an act of trust in the belief that what you pay attention to shapes your reality, what you invest time in shapes your experience, and what you develop in you and through you impacts your world for good or for ill.

> Tithing your time is an act of trust in the belief that what you pay attention to shapes your reality, what you invest time in shapes your experience, and what you develop in you and through you impacts your world for good or for ill.

Tithing your time is a counterintuitive act of trust in the belief that taking time away from the pressing needs of your work to reflect on your life actually increases your productivity and effectiveness.

Tithing your time is an act of trust in the belief that as you spend it in self-reflection and self-evaluation, you actually increase your time capacity, not diminish it.

Tithing your time is an act of trust in the belief that as you model time management by prioritizing reflection you are empowering those around you to act in that same kind of trust for themselves. You are creating a transformational ripple effect in the world.

Tithing your time is an act of trust in the belief that this practice develops in you the ability to be more fully present every moment, more fully alive in every circumstance, more fully human in every encounter.

In Thornton Wilder's play *Our Town*, the lead character, a young woman named Emily, dies in childbirth. The Stage Manager gives her a unique opportunity—she is allowed to return from death and spend one day of her life with her family and friends. She has high hopes for that day but ends up being bitterly disappointed. Just before returning to her grave, she bemoans to the Stage Manager, "We don't have time to look at one another. [She breaks down sobbing.] I didn't realize. So all that was going on and we never noticed ... Do any human beings ever realize life while they live it—every, every minute?"

He replies, "No. The saints and poets, maybe—they do some."[46]

Poets and other artists certainly need this kind of awareness to write, paint, draw, or compose with any authenticity and impact. They learn the art of paying attention to everything around and within them. They develop the ability to see beyond what's in front of them—to notice the nuances, the colors, the variety, the diversity. They are experts in looking below the surface to the deeper world.

But here's the thing. Artists aren't the only ones who need to practice this capacity to grasp life deeply. We are all artists of sorts, artists of our own lives. Every day we are painting scenes and portraits portraying our perspectives of life. And if we are to live authentically, as we all truly can, we must join the saints and poets and learn the art of living deeply.

Maybe you will want to begin tithing your time to include some "painting"—self-portraits, landscapes, group scenes all from your life and world—paintings that reveal more than just the superficial. Why not develop the art of knowing yourself more deeply and, then, of showing up more authentically everywhere you go. It's time to schedule some strategic stops.

PERSONAL PAUSES

❚❚ Regular transformational self-reflection thrives in specific time and location. When, how often, and where can you set aside intentional opportunities for self-reflection? Identify those three details right now. The following steps you can do during your self-reflection times.

❚❚ Take the emotional intelligence assessment to discover your current score for self-awareness, self-regulation, social awareness, and social regulation (from Travis Bradbury & Jean Greaves, *Emotional Intelligence 2.0*). The assessment results chart your best path forward for raising your scores in each of those four areas.

❚❚ Using the list of feeling words (from http://www.psychpage. com/learning/library/assess/feelings.html), identify what feeling you had in your latest conflict with someone. Start becoming familiar with these words and when they show up in your day-to-day life at home and at work.

❚❚ Identify what steps you can take to transition your feelings from what you felt in that conflict to a place of more peace and contentment.

TEAM PAUSES

|| Begin a team session with the following sharing question using the list of feeling words: "Which word on this list have you recently felt? What was happening that stimulated this feeling for you?"

|| Have everyone on the team take the emotional intelligence assessment (from Travis Bradbury & Jean Greaves, *Emotional Intelligence 2.0*). Share one or two results with everyone on the team in a team session and what step you will take to improve those results.

|| Team sharing question: "Describe a time at work when you felt really strong and energized." If you have already taken the CliftonStrengths assessment, share one of your top five strengths and how you have used that strength recently.

|| Practice (and pay attention) to fast thinking vs. slow thinking. Talk about the differences you notice. Identify when it's most effective to lean into slow thinking instead of fast thinking. Delineate when you will have a team time that utilizes slow thinking and what you will do during that time to tap into slow thinking. Plan the session.

Shift Limiting Beliefs

Dr. Chris Argyris, a business theorist at Harvard Business School, spent years studying how organizations and people respond to obstacles that appear in their paths. He noticed there are two ways people tend to learn.

The most common he called "single loop learning." When something goes wrong, or a difficulty appears, this is about applying the typical rules and policies as effectively as possible. If that doesn't work, you change your tactics or strategy. It's more of a "let's tweak what we're doing" approach.

The less common but ultimately more effective approach Argyris called "double loop learning." Instead of applying the rules or tweaking the process, this is about changing the rules. It is about being willing to evaluate the underlying assumptions and biases that have been operating sometimes even unconsciously and then changing them to be more effective. Instead of tweaking, it deconstructs, dismantles the current process, in order to build something completely new and better.

"This more psychologically nuanced self-examination requires that we honestly challenge our beliefs and summon the courage to act on that information, which may lead to fresh ways of thinking about our lives and our goals."[47]

Remember the story about tennis player Martina Navratilova? When she lost that famous match with Chris Evert, she didn't simply consider how she might be using the wrong grip on her racket. She didn't simply tell herself she needed to practice her game more. She didn't simply decide to tweak her body positions and postures and playing style. All of those strategies would have been single loop learning.

Instead, she chose to take the more courageous and transformational approach. She hired new professionals to help her completely deconstruct her entire game of tennis. From top to bottom, she re-evaluated, broke down her game piece by piece, and then reconstructed her whole mental and physical approach to tennis. She challenged her assumptions like, "I can get by on talent and instinct alone." All of this is double loop learning. And the result was a game-changer.

Truth is, you cannot have self-awareness without also engaging in honest self-evaluation.

> Truth is, you cannot have self-awareness without also engaging in honest self-evaluation.

So let's talk about what this kind of self-evaluation looks like. The stakes might not be as high for you and me as they were for Navratilova. But the future of our personal and professional success and well-being depends on our choice to engage in honest self-evaluation. The process I engaged in after leading that team session described in the last chapter showed me the value of this approach. And for it to be effective, as Dr. Argyris says, it must include evaluating our beliefs and biases and assumptions—identifying which beliefs are limiting and based upon false assumptions, those that are no longer serving us, and those which we simply need to let go in order to replace with empowering truths.

3. Engaging in Honest Self-Evaluation

Here are some questions as you engage in self-evaluation—whether for the purpose of understanding what triggers you and how to best respond, or as an after-project debrief to help you learn how to improve:

1. What am I feeling right now? How is my body responding?

Learn how to put words to your feelings. Are you sad, angry, jealous, insecure, anxious, uncertain, discouraged, depressed, threatened? If you search online for "feeling words," you'll find a whole list that can help you put words to what you're experiencing.[48] I've used this list with clients who are having difficulty describing their feelings. Many of us have simply not grown up in family cultures that are articulate with emotional vocabulary. The list helps provide feeling labels.

Your goal is to be able to put a word to what you're feeling at any given moment, and especially when you're being triggered by someone or something.

I knew at those moments in my managers session that I was feeling discomfort from feeling threatened. Because I was leading the session, I didn't have the time to nuance that feeling. All I knew was that my body was reacting like it does when I'm under increased stress—my mouth got dry, my heartrate went up, my voice started to get unsteady—until I realized it and quickly compensated. The message was clear: I'm feeling stressed.

When I had more time to evaluate the situation, I realized I was feeling intimidated, which led me to feel insecure (that I wasn't good enough). And later on that evening, I spiraled into feelings of inadequacy, uncertainty, and ultimately doom and gloom, which led to discouragement, fear of the future, and hopelessness.

The point is, unless you know what you're feeling, you don't know what to do with it or how to respond to it in healthy ways. So many people simply pass over the feeling—they stuff it or sweep it under the rug. But emotions always have a way of coming out into the open, often in painful ways.

> Feelings are messengers—their purpose is to help us understand something important going on at the time.

2. What do I tend to do with my feelings?

It's one thing to identify your feelings. It's another thing to learn how to manage them, to deal with them constructively and effectively.

To be able do this, you have to acknowledge this truth: feelings are not good or bad, feelings are simply feelings. In fact, as experts remind us, feelings are messengers—their purpose is to help us understand something important going on at the time, like, "I'm feeling _____ because this person/situation/circumstance is really important to me. If it weren't important to me, I wouldn't be feeling this."

Here's why this is significant:

"The downfall of attaching such labels [as in good or bad feelings] to your emotions is that judging your emotions keeps you from really understanding what it is that you are feeling. When you allow yourself to sit with an emotion and become fully aware of it, you can understand what is causing it. Suspending judgment of emotions allows them to run their course and vanish. Passing judgment on whether you should or shouldn't be feeling what you are feeling just heaps more emotions on top of the pile and prevents the original feeling from running its course ... Refrain from putting it into the good or bad pile and remind yourself that the feeling is there to help you understand something important."[49]

So your goal is to embrace the feeling, not to judge it. Don't beat yourself up about it or sweep it under the rug if it's a difficult or painful feeling; instead, identify it by putting an accurate word to it. Then, let it be—let yourself feel the feeling. Then you can explore what that feeling is trying to tell you. What is important to you that is needing attention?

In my debriefing of my coaching session and its aftermath, I realized that my feelings of insecurity and inadequacy both during and after were messengers telling me that

- I valued the opinions of the leaders in that group.
- I had upped the stakes in my mind of the importance of this session because they were present.
- Doing really well mattered to me because I hoped it might lead to openings to other teams in the company.
- When I felt challenged by a couple of them, I was afraid I was losing my credibility, and thus my influence.

Now the question was, what was I going to do about it?

3. What are my underlying biases, assumptions, and limiting beliefs driving my feelings and behaviors? Where are these feelings coming from? And what am I going to do about them?

Central to your process of bringing yourself back to a place of contentment, joy, and hope is to evaluate where your feelings are coming from. What is triggering them? Why are your internal buttons getting pushed?

This has to involve evaluating your assumptions and beliefs, asking "Why?" and "Is this true?" This is always a challenging step for us because it's not simple, it's not quick, and it takes intentionality and time. A strategic stop is required. The good news is that with practice, it can take place more quickly and efficiently.

Martina Navratilova realized, upon reflection, that she had been operating under the belief (assumption) that her natural abilities were enough to take her to the top of the tennis world. She just needed to practice more, to utilize those abilities more effectively.

But that was a faulty assumption, a limiting belief, that led to a negative outcome. Though she had tremendous natural abilities, she still needed to embed strategic knowledge and the development of completely new abilities within her natural style. And further, in her deconstruction of her current game, it became clear that her natural abilities had actually included some bad habits that were keeping her from excelling to her full potential. She needed to break these habits and form new, more effective ones.

Truth is, our biases, beliefs, and assumptions help to create our responses (feelings) to people and situations. So unless we challenge beliefs and biases—evaluate them carefully—we'll never know how they're shaping our feelings and we'll never know where our feelings are originating. And then we'll never manage those feelings effectively.

There's an ancient proverb that says, "As a person thinks in their heart, so are they." Our beliefs shape our behavior and, ultimately, our outcomes.

Leaders and teams need to intentionally go through a debrief and evaluation process to learn from their experience what to improve next time. And this must include how biases and beliefs of people in the group, including the leader, have impacted the experience and outcome. Without this kind of process, the same dynamics will be repeated over and over again to the detriment of the team.

> Our beliefs shape our behavior and, ultimately, our outcomes.

I can guarantee that if you make these kinds of discoveries and then identify and choose to practice a new way of being in those triggering moments, it will change the game of your life.

4. What is working well in my life these days, and what isn't working as well as I would like?

For decades now, the U.S. military has been using what they refer to as AARs—After Action Reviews. They are rigorous in deconstructing what exactly happened and how it went; based on that information, they determine what they could do next time to improve the process and outcome.

Here's the way Tom Deierlein, cofounder and CEO at ThunderCat Technology and veteran of the Iraq war, describes it:

"When I was in Baghdad, we did an After Action Review after every mission. Thirty minutes after we got back inside the wire. Every mission. Why? It kept us focused, it allowed us to reflect. It forced us to improve each and every day. The stakes were high. Mistakes and flaws in execution get people killed so people actually looked forward to them. Many units would have them during the beginning of the tour, then get comfortable, lazy, and stop. Big mistake. Maybe you are getting better, but how about sharing best practices with those who will follow in your footsteps? We had an expression in combat—'Complacency Kills.'"[50]

He said it was a very simple process. Everyone would go around the circle and share three things that went well and three things that didn't go well. If someone covered one of your three, it wouldn't be able to be repeated. You would have to come up with a new learning. They would keep it fast paced, writing everyone's observations down, and making sure everyone's recommendations were understood. That was it. Simple. Powerful.

We might not have the same stakes in our everyday lives as an active military unit in combat. But nonetheless, the quality of our lives is at stake—whether we want to live fully alive and thriving in well-being or whether we want to simply exist in the status quo, drifting along, in a diminished state. Our choice.

When is the last time you actually asked yourself those questions? Imagine if you took the time to regularly reflect and evaluate how things are going.

What is going well? What isn't going so well? What do you need to change to improve? What have you learned lately?

Who are you? How are you wired—what is your authentic human design? What makes you unique from others? What are your strengths? What are your weaknesses or areas for improvement? What do you want to celebrate about yourself? What concerns do you need to pay attention to? What are the shadow sides that tend to show up that impede your progress and positive presence? What beliefs are limiting you instead of empowering you? What changes do you need to make to be more healthy and alive, thriving with more vitality? What kind of influence are you having on others? Do people around you feel fully alive and empowered because of you, or do they feel diminished?

This depth of self-evaluation cannot take place while you're jetting to back-to-back appointments. This takes thought—at least, if you want to be genuinely honest and authentic and actually grow from it. Nothing short of carving out strategic stops can glean the value from this reflection.

It doesn't have to consume hours (although deeper self-evaluations could take longer). Engaging in a few targeted minutes can produce meaningful learning. If you choose to develop a regular practice and ask yourself some of these strategic questions, you will take this step to a transformational level.

In my processing of the managers coaching session—reflecting on my feelings and evaluating my process, beliefs, biases, and assumptions—I came to some very significant understandings about myself that not only pulled me out of the pit but launched me into a renewed spirit of liberation, empowerment, confidence, and excitement. I made connections between some of my long-held beliefs since childhood and my limiting beliefs, connections that I never knew were there. It was convicting to realize that some of these beliefs were no longer serving me. And it was freeing to give myself permission to let them go.

It's true, the deconstruction process is scary at times and certainly challenging. But if we want to grow into our human potential, we cannot neglect this internal work.

Because I had a regular ritual and practice in place—a built-in strategic stop—I was able to spend the necessary time to reflect and evaluate where I was at and where I needed to go internally and externally. And I went through this with my wife, who is my most valued partner and the one who knows me better than anyone else.

Dealing with Our Limiting Beliefs

My wife and I read a book some years ago that talked about the seven self-limiting beliefs that we all have in one ranking or another: I am not safe, I am worthless, I am powerless, I am not lovable, I cannot trust anyone, I am bad, I am alone.[51] We each tend to rate highest in one or two.

Self-limiting beliefs are emotionally charged stories or narratives that are often rooted in traumatic experiences in our childhoods. Through the years, we fine-tune these stories so expertly that they turn into hardcore beliefs about ourselves that end up impacting everything we experience later on in life. And we believe them to be completely true. They become the lens through which we interpret life.

> Self-limiting beliefs are emotionally charged stories or narratives that are often rooted in traumatic experiences in our childhoods. Through the years, we fine-tune these stories so expertly that they turn into hardcore beliefs about ourselves that end up impacting everything we experience later on in life.

So that whenever we end up having a micro-traumatic experience, the beliefs kick in and what is called traumatic resonance occurs. In other words, we relive the pain without even thinking about the original trauma. And the pain can be both physiological and emotional.

Neuroscientists, with the help of brain imaging technology (fMRIs), can actually see that neural networks and synapses continue to be formed around these limiting beliefs. Every time we embrace these stories and accept them as true, the neural networks strengthen. And as a result, these narratives become solidified and assumed to be true.

Notice each of those limiting beliefs begin with the words, "I am ..." These beliefs are a statement of self-identity. "I am" means that this is our basic nature—it's who we, are not just what we do. No wonder they are so destructive to our lives.

In the course of reading the book, my wife and I journaled answers to questions revolving around where our identified limiting beliefs might have come from and been reinforced growing up. What stories come to mind? What were we feeling in those stories? How were those early conclusions reinforced through the years?

My recollections were almost instantaneous. Without even trying, my mind went immediately to two childhood stories.

In the first memory, I was five or six years old. My dad was capturing this on Super 8 movies, so I remember it vividly because I've watched it many times through the years. My family was getting ready to get in the car and go for a drive. My older brother and younger sister were on the sidewalk leading to the driveway, dressed nicely for the trip. I was wearing a blazer jacket, which Mom obviously had not intended for me to wear. She wanted me in a sweater like the one my brother had obediently put on. Dad's camera was filming as Mom came over to me, sweater in hand, and began to take off my jacket. In the home movie, you can see me desperately fighting the removal, jumping around and refusing to let her take off my jacket. She worked harder. I resisted harder. But finally I lost the battle. Jacket removed, Mom proceeded to put the sweater on me. You can see the look on my face—one of complete defeat.

Now this doesn't seem to be anything really spectacular or traumatic, right? I mean, this could be a scene from almost any family. But what counts here is what I was feeling at the time. It's as clear to me now as it was then. I remember feeling completely defeated. Angry. Like my desires didn't count. I felt powerless to act on my behalf. What I wanted apparently didn't matter.

Memory two. I'm in college. Home for a weekend, I'm sitting around the table with Mom and Dad after dinner. I'm regaling them with all the new, stimulating ideas and theology I've been learning from my theology and religion classes. I'm trying to impress them with my radical views like young adults are inclined to enjoy doing with their parents—pushing their buttons knowingly by stretching beliefs, arguing, and debating against their more traditional beliefs.

After about 10 minutes of this debate, Dad finally stands up and walks away. He never really liked conflict or debating. It all becomes too much for him and he retreats to another room.

Mom always enjoyed a stimulating conversation. So she hangs in there for quite a while, asking questions, pressing her perspectives, pushing back on my views. And when it is time to end, she summarizes her views, drives her point home, and essentially states that her belief is the right one. And I should be very careful about what I allow myself to believe. She is right. I am wrong. Again.

I remember feeling that evening that, when expressing my excitement over learning, my own views don't really count. Dad leaves the conversation early. And Mom always wins in the end. Apparently what I believe doesn't really matter. End of discussion.

It seems like a pretty harmless experience. Again, this scene happens in many families, especially when we become young adults. But the message that my brain told me, in resonance with my earlier childhood story, was that I am powerless on my own. What I want isn't good. I can't rely on my own wisdom or knowledge or capacity. I need outside authority to always make the decisions or choices for me.

"I am not powerful or capable on my own."

And a huge portion of my life was shaped by that self-limiting belief. It's an "I am" statement—a statement of being. It's not just, "I act powerless at times," or "I sometimes feel powerless," or "I was not powerful that one time." The moment we use "I am," we're describing an identity, a piece of what we believe to be inherently true about our very nature.

And this self-limiting belief states that my inherent nature is that I am not powerful and not capable on my own. What I want isn't as important as obeying what those above me think is right for me. I need to rely on the authority of others rather than my own. I can't trust myself and my own desires. I must always acquiesce to a higher authority. And like for many of us growing up in a religious environment, the highest authority is always God, but interpreted, of course, by human leaders above us.

No wonder these beliefs are so influential in shaping our responses to life. Our personal narrative is that we inherently are these limitations. So we end up giving away our own agency and caving in to other people's opinions or views of us and of the world. We have essentially lost ourselves to a false narrative.

The results are destructive:

- our sense of helplessness increases (victim mentality),
- along with corresponding stress,
- often with corresponding cortisol in our systems,
- which damages our health and internal organs,
- which short-circuits peace and contentment and creativity,
- which makes us less capable of having loving, trusting relationships,
- which isolates us and leads to higher loneliness,
- and which, in turn, recycles the stress and cortisol responses.

The cycle is vicious and never-ending. All stemming from adopting a false narrative—a self-limiting belief—about whom we really are.

The good news is that I don't have to stay in the shadow of my limiting belief. Neither do you. I can challenge it. I can turn it into an empowering belief that tells the truth about me.

"I am powerful and capable!"

When I came to this discovery, I turned it into a daily, sometimes hourly, mantra, repeating it again and again. "I am powerful and capable!"

By doing this, we are rewiring the neural networks in our brains. Here's the way it works, according to Drs. Pratt and Lambrou:

"This is how we form beliefs: we literally grow them, like a dynamic topiary of the mind. The resulting beliefs are stronger than feelings, deeper than thoughts. Beliefs are patterns of thought so ingrained in our neural networks they have become automatic, like entrenched habits of thinking. They are the bedrock of our psychological architecture."[52]

So go ahead, entrench yourself in the truth about who you truly are. Restate. Restate. Restate your right belief. Ingrain this narrative in your neural networks. Make it a new habit and pattern of thinking.

And open the door to liberation and transformation.

Liberating Ourselves from our Limiting Beliefs

Did you have any specific nightmares as a kid?

I sure did! One in particular. A real doozy for little Greggie. Gorillas. Big ones, like King Kong. And they were always coming to eat me. How this relates to my limiting belief will become apparent in a moment.

What made them so terrifying was that whenever the nightmare would wake me up, I would always hear the gorilla right in my room. I would be petrified and paralyzed. I'd want so desperately to run down the short hallway to Mom and Dad's room. But I couldn't. If I got out of bed, surely the gorilla would catch me and devour me.

Often, as Mom would later tell me, she would be awakened in the middle of the night feeling a presence beside her bed. Little Greggie standing there, white as a ghost, shaking from fear, having escaped the gorilla in his room.

"It's all right, Greggie. You're all right. There's no gorilla in your room. You're safe."

And sometimes she would walk me back to my bed and together we would look under the bed and in the closet.

"See, Greggie? There's no gorilla here. You're just having a bad dream. You're okay, son! Now let's put you back to bed. It was just a bad dream."

I discovered later one night that instead of the sound of a gorilla in my room, what I was actually hearing was the sound of my dad's loud snoring storming down the hallway and assaulting my environment. Phew! No gorilla after all.

And yet the nightmares continued. For many years.

Many decades later, when my wife and I were in the process of working through our limiting beliefs, I came upon another truth in a book I was reading that crystallized my new empowering belief—"I am powerful and capable!"

The authors described working with a professional client who was totally unable to deal with his anxiety and fears about working with people who had lots of authority and power. He felt intimidated. Afraid. Which made him timid and incapable of showing up with confidence.

In exploring the roots of this debilitating fear, he ended up telling them about being bullied by kids on the playground when he was a child. And how after that trauma, he started having nightmares about being attacked by lions.

The psychotherapists explored with him, "What does the lion represent to you?"

He thought about it and replied, "It's something I'm really, really afraid of. It's what intimidates me. I'm afraid of people who are powerful and assertive."

"What if," they posited to him, "what if actually the lion represents a part of you that was wanting to come out when you were being bullied? What if in fact you are powerful like a lion and that part of you is wanting to show up and give you your own power?"

Parents want to help their kids feel better. So when their kids have nightmares, parents often simply assure them, "It's okay. There's no gorilla. There's no lion. See? Nothing here. You're okay. You'll be fine."

And as a result, we end up disassociating ourselves from a real, significant part of ourselves that wants to be an ally to us, that wants to empower us, to show us our strengths and power.

Like I did with my gorilla.

When I read this, I experienced an extremely encouraging epiphany. It led to a transformational liberation. I immediately resonated all the way into my inner core. I felt it that moment.

I am a gorilla. I am powerful and capable on my own.

The gorilla had come to me, even as a child, to help me see a really important part of myself. It was wanting to come out. It knew I was needing this part of myself to give me self-confidence and courage.

For what? Do you know when these nightmares started? Not very long after that scene of disempowerment I had with my mom over my blazer jacket.

The gorilla part of me showed up wanting to assure me that I was never a victim. That I had the power. That I was capable on my own. That I had agency. That my voice counts, always.

Unfortunately, I never made that connection when I was a child. I wasn't taught how to see this nightmarish gorilla. And so I disassociated myself from that huge part of me. It was something to be afraid of. For decades.

I felt that disconnect. And I often struggled with myself about my sense of lack of personal power, authority, and agency. I often felt intimidated by people of power and authority. I faked it really well on the outside. But inside I felt it. And I know it hampered my confidence and ability.

Until I finally became liberated by the truth of who I really am. And that realization, this new story, this true narrative, has radically empowered me into being more authentically me—a man of true power, capacity, boldness, confidence, and a fiercely expressive protector and nurturer of my tribe.

Bringing Our Parts Back Together Again

This is why taking deliberate and intentional strategic stops is so vital. This isn't just some luxury to engage in when there's nothing more important or urgent. This is the only way you and I can look squarely at ourselves and ask the important and often challenging questions. Strategic stops are the recovery moments when we grow and develop into our truest and best selves.

The question is, do you have the courage to take regular strategic stops for the purpose of self-reflection, to place yourself on a journey of personal development and growth so you can show up in

> Strategic stops are the recovery moments when we grow and develop into our truest and best selves.

the world as your authentic and powerful self, to honestly evaluate what is working for you and what is not and why—what limiting beliefs might be holding you back from living your liberated self? How might all the various parts of you be brought back together again into one unified self, resulting in being fully alive?

Have you heard the story of the European explorer in Africa who was trekking with a large group of African porters who were carrying all the equipment and luggage? He noticed that every few days they would stop and refuse to pick up all the loads to get started again. Getting frustrated, he demanded to know why. The tribal leader said, "They're letting their souls catch up to their bodies."

In today's fast-faced, nonstop culture, all the parts of ourselves get divided and separated from each other. So we live in disconnection and end up paying the price.

Until, like these African porters, we realize what's happening and refuse to stay in the rat race. So we stop—in a strategic stop—to let all our parts catch up with each other so that we can live in genuine alignment, authenticity, and wholeness.

Self-reflection and evaluation and work are not enemies. They are partners. I can guarantee you that when you build regular strategic stops into your schedule for the purpose of shifting your limiting beliefs into empowering ones, your work vastly improves. And when you're involved in meaningful, purposeful work that utilizes strategic stops of refocusing and reconnecting along the way, you and everyone around you benefit.

The strategic stop is your path to being more fully alive and more fully human. Ignore at your own peril.

PERSONAL PAUSES

❚❚ What is working well (and/or feeling well) in your life these days, and what isn't working very well (and/or not feeling very well)? Make a list of several things in each category.

❚❚ Which of the seven limiting beliefs (I am not safe, I am worthless, I am powerless, I am not lovable, I cannot trust anyone, I am bad, I am alone) tends to impact you the most? Describe some stories in your life (as early as childhood) that tapped into that limiting belief.

❚❚ How could you reframe (reword) that limiting belief into an empowering belief? For example, "I am powerless" (limiting belief) to "I am powerful" (empowering belief). Repeat that empowering statement multiple times during the day.

❚❚ What is an assumption you made about someone or a situation that ended up not being true? For future reference, how could you avoid making that automatic assumption? When you're tempted to jump to a conclusion, ask yourself, "What else could be true here?" and "What is my responsibility in this?"

TEAM PAUSES

❚❚ Engage in an AAR (After Action Review) team session. Have everyone answer the questions: What three things went well, and what three things didn't go so well? If someone covers one of someone else's three, it can't be repeated. The person has to come up with a new learning. Keep it fast paced, writing down everyone's observations, and make sure everyone's recommendations are understood. Debrief the experience.

❚❚ As a team, talk about single loop learning vs. double loop learning. Describe times when both have happened recently and pros and cons.

❚❚ Team sharing questions: How has one of your limiting beliefs about yourself shown up in your interaction with the team? What impact did it have on the team? How would your corresponding empowering belief impact the team?

❚❚ Discuss as a team how the pace at work impacts your choice to set aside regular strategic stops for reflection and evaluation. Identify one step you can take to alter this pace.

Sharpen Strengths

A man was speaking at a religious service in a nursing home. He wanted to present something comforting to the aging patients. So he began by saying, "You belong!"

He was about to continue when a 90-year-old woman in a wheelchair startled him by shouting in her high, wheezy voice, "To whom?"

Classic question. This is one of the most fundamental needs of all human beings. To feel a sense of belonging. To be connected with others who share your life in some meaningful ways. To feel that you matter. That you have value. That you are included. That you are necessary. That you have something to offer that will be recognized and appreciated.

Sebastian Junger, in his book *Tribe: On Homecoming and Belonging*, observes, "Humans don't mind hardship, in fact, they thrive on it; what they mind is not feeling necessary. Modern society has perfected the art of making people not feel necessary."

I have been a keen observer of human behavior my entire professional life—what motivates people, what inspires people, what empowers people, what obstacles keep people from engaging meaningfully and purposefully in life and work.

And I'm equally interested in what happens when you bring individuals together into groups that form organizations. What motivates people in those environments, what inspires and empowers them, what keeps them from being fully engaged, what produces high-performing and innovative teams?

Here's one of the things I've learned through the years. If the fundamental need of every human being is to belong, to feel both connected and useful, then for an organization (which is fundamentally a collection of human beings around a specific cause and mission) to be effective, it must be a place where people thrive and are fully engaged in that mission and where they feel necessary. For that to happen, the leaders must prioritize creating opportunities for everyone to experience the fulfillment of these needs.

My bias is that the most important resource of any organization is not the stakeholders or the finances or the organizational chart or the physical space housing it or the location or its marketing or even its innovative products and outputs—as important as all those facets are. The most important resource is pure and simple the human beings within the organization. No people, no organization.

So my questions to every leader within organizations are, what are you doing with your most important resource? How are you developing them? How are you building them? How are you mobilizing them? How are you empowering and motivating them? How are you protecting them? How are you multiplying them?

> Almost 80 percent of employees describe themselves as disengaged from their work and workplaces.

Here is the sobering reality of contemporary organizational climate. Gallup has conducted the largest workplace studies in the world and reveals a staggering picture:

- Almost 80 percent of employees describe themselves as disengaged from their work and workplaces.[53] That means they're showing up with very little energy and enthusiasm on the job, little to no loyalty to the organization, and next to no buy-in to the company vision and mission. They are simply going through the motions in order to get a paycheck.
- As a result, companies are spending billions of dollars every year in re-training because of their inability to retain workers.

This certainly doesn't seem to be the epitome of effective resource management—human or otherwise. Though almost every organization states that it supports the value of every employee or worker, these results indicate the truth: they are not practicing what they preach. Saying it is one thing, facilitating it is another.

Motivating the People Around You

One of the significant human motivation paradigms is the Self-Determination Theory. It's based upon our intrinsic motivations (as opposed to extrinsic). For people to feel truly motivated to do something, to invest their hearts and souls into something, they need to feel and experience these four components[54]:

1. **Competence**—the ability to control the outcome of an activity and experience mastery of that task, utilizing our unique strengths
2. **Authenticity**—the desire to be an independent agent in our own lives in a way that is authentically us
3. **Connectedness**—the universal need to be connected to and experience caring for others
4. **Psychological Safety**—the need to feel safe for interpersonal risk-taking within a climate of mutual trust and respect

These four powerful motivators are non-negotiables if a leader wants to develop an organizational environment that leverages and maximizes its human resources.

Here's the way this looks in a diagram:

THE FOUR FACTORS OF INNOVATIVE ENGAGEMENT

If you're a leader or manager, how are you tapping into these four motivators within yourself? Within your people? If you're an individual contributor and team member, how are you paying attention to developing in yourself these four motivators for effective living and working? If you're a parent, how are you developing these motivations in your children? If you're a pastor or spiritual leader, how are you speaking to and helping to establish these motivations in your attendees and community members?

My coaching and training work with leaders and teams revolves around these four motivations. The activities I facilitate and the processes I coach focus on developing competency, authenticity and autonomy, and connectedness within each person and each team.

Let's talk about shaping strategic stops for this foundational process. We'll look carefully at the first two motivations. The third will be addressed in the next chapter.

1. Developing Competency

"Tell a story about a recent time you felt really, really strong. You felt highly energized, powerful, fulfilled. What specifically were you doing?"

That's a question I ask every person to share the answer to in our team sessions. I'm always fascinated to hear people's personal stories. And the whole team enjoys hearing everyone's verbal pictures, too.

One of the team members in a session said, "My girlfriend and I were driving out in the middle of nowhere when my car broke down. I'm not much of a mechanic. But I'm a learner. So I got my cell phone and Googled the car symptoms. There were a number of posts about what my car was manifesting. I opened up YouTube and started watching some videos about how to address the problem. One of the clips suggested a specific, rather simple solution, which I then tried. And lo and behold, it worked. I started up the engine, closed the hood, and with a look of triumph got into the car. My girlfriend looked at me as though I were Superman. 'You're my hero!' she said as we drove away. I had this amazing feeling inside—I felt really strong and energized. I loved it! I could do that kind of stuff all day long!"

The look on his face while he told this story was priceless—smiling, beaming, obviously proud of what he had done. And I looked at the others around the table—smiling, nodding, impressed.

Everyone needs to feel competent at something.

There are two kinds of competence: unconscious competence and conscious competence. Unconscious competence is being good at something without thinking about it or maybe not ever realizing it. You're simply good at some things. It comes so naturally for you that you probably don't spend much time thinking about. It's instinctive. If this kind of competence remains unconscious to you, it has a built-in limit to it.

> Everyone needs to feel competent at something.

But the moment you bring your competence into consciousness and awareness—when you know why you're competent, how you are doing that competent behavior, what it is that makes you competent—you can increase your competence exponentially because you know exactly what you can do to increase it.

Here's the way Marcus Buckingham, one of the most well-known voices in the strengths movement, puts it:

"Although you have undoubtedly experienced some moments of success and fulfillment in your life, the secret to strong living lies in being able to replicate these moments time and again. To do this you need to understand these moments deeply. You need to discern which strengths were in play and how they combined to create either the performance or the satisfaction or both."[55]

He's talking about the necessity of developing conscious competence.

My goal with people is to help them increase their conscious competence. That's why I like to use that opening sharing question. It helps people make the mental and emotional connection between the feelings of strength and energy and certain behaviors.

"When I use my Learner strength—when I tap into my curiosity by using YouTube to help me figure out a problem and what to do about it—I feel really energized and strong." That's increasing conscious competence. And when that connection is made, this person can then determine other ways or arenas in which this strength can be used even more strategically and in a more optimized way. The growth is almost limitless.

This is why one of the tools I enjoy using the most in my work with leaders and teams is Gallup's CliftonStrengths assessment.[56] It measures the brain's natural preferences—those behaviors you engage in that make you feel strong, energized, and fulfilled. When combined with knowledge about these preferences (what they mean, how can they be used effectively) and skill development (regularly practicing the use of the preferences), they are turned into strengths. These are your places of highest natural energy, power, effectiveness, and greatest fulfillment.

Here's why this tool is so valuable in this conversation about personal competency. Not only does it identify your top strengths, it also informs you of what makes you unique from everyone else. Though you may share certain strengths with other people, there is a 1:33 million chance that someone else has your same top five in the same order as you.[57] And then you add the next five strengths—rounding out your top 10, which are your primary natural preferences—and the ratio jumps off the charts.

In other words, no one else can do exactly what you can do in the same way as you. You are incredibly unique, able to fill a role in a style and manner that few others can. That's why, as I tell every team member I work with, unless you show up with conscious intentionality in the fullness of all your top strengths, the team will be deprived of a contribution that only you can provide. And you owe it to your team and to your leaders to provide your very best. If everyone on the team shows up this way, the team becomes a powerhouse of amazing skill and incredible productivity, and they enjoy the process along the way.

> "People who know and use their strengths are 6X as likely to be engaged at work, 7.8% more productive in their role, 3X as likely to have an excellent quality of life, and 6X as likely to do what they do best every day."

Here's the good news, in case all of this sounds a bit daunting to you. It's to your own self-interest and benefit to discover and learn how to leverage your strengths, your best competencies. Do you know why? Here's the research:

"People who know and use their strengths are 6X as likely to be engaged at work, 7.8% more productive in their role, 3X as likely to have an excellent quality of life, and 6X as likely to do what they do best every day."[58]

Imagine those benefits in your everyday life at home and at work. Who wouldn't want to experience these outcomes!

And if you're a manager and leader, imagine having not just you but all your teams experiencing these results. Who wouldn't want to see this in the people you oversee? Everybody wins this way.

So remember, leader: when you help your employees develop a sense of competency—a basic human need—you are providing them with one of the four powerful motivators in their lives, equipping them to be fully engaged, fulfilled, and productive every day.

We all have a need to feel competent, to know that we can make a useful contribution to whatever context we're in. This is part of what it means to be human.

2. Developing Authenticity

I remember well a comment my mom made to me when I was 11 or 12. We were standing in my bedroom after having made my bed in the morning. She looked around the room, noticing the difference between my older brother's space and mine. Then she observed, "I wish you could be more organized like your brother."

I remember looking around the room, trying to figure out what she might be referring to. My area was pretty clean—I always made my bed and picked up my clothes. My other things were put away in their proper place. So I was a bit confused.

"Might she be talking about my scheduling or my time management?" I thought to myself. "Maybe I could be more productive if I organized my life better?"

I don't remember her ever specifying her meaning. It seemed like a fairly harmless, though confusing, comment. But as it turned out, that view of me became embedded in my psyche and identity for several decades. I always thought of myself as lacking the skill of good, effective organization. I simply figured, "Hey, organizational management just isn't me; it's not my thing."

And then one evening in my late twenties, I was visiting with the head elder of my congregation, who was a wise older man and like a father figure to me as a young pastor. We were having a high-level conversation about strategic planning and re-organizing the church for more effective member mobilization.

At one point, I said, "Well, the challenge is that organization just isn't my thing. It's not one of my strengths. I suck at it! In fact ..."

He immediately stopped me midsentence and said, "Greg, I never want to hear you say that about yourself again!"

His firmness surprised me. I didn't know what to make of it. "Why not?" I asked.

He went on. "That is not a true statement about yourself. And it isn't serving you to continue reinforcing that false belief. I've heard you say this before, too."

And then for the next 10 minutes, he described all the ways he had observed me engaging in strategic and efficient administration and organizational leadership the last few years.

He ended by saying, "So I never want to hear you say that about yourself again. It's simply not true!"

That was a profound turning point in my life. He was stating an identity I had always thought I never had—and he skillfully backed it up with impressive illustrations and proof.

He was challenging my faulty sense of authenticity and autonomy. I had lived for years believing what my mom had said with her comparison between my older brother and me.

Because he gave such undeniable proof of this unknown piece of me, it landed for me. It felt authentic and true the more I thought and reflected about it. And it shifted my whole self-identity. Over the next few decades of pastoring, I served congregations in ways that gave further evidence of the truth that I actually have great abilities and strengths in strategic and administrative organization. I had not accessed them before because I had an inauthentic view of myself. But the moment my dear friend spoke truth to me, my paradigm shifted 180 degrees. And that shift unlocked a deep and more authentic place in me, which in turn opened up new vistas and destinies for me.

Our place of greatest personal power and influence is in authenticity. Living authentically gives us our greatest autonomy—our ability to embrace agency and self-efficacy instead of letting others dictate who we are—and our greatest capacity to achieve our potential in spite of obstacles and constraints that so many people try to put on us.

> Our place of greatest personal power and influence is in authenticity.

Seventeenth century Dutch philosopher Baruch Spinoza framed it this way: "To be what we are, and to become what we are capable of becoming, is the only end of life."

What the paradigm of self-determination states is that authenticity and autonomy are transformational motivators for human beings. We are driven by the quest to discover our most authentic and true selves. We are longing and hungering for this truth. Without it, we drift at times aimlessly in a futile attempt to know our place in the world and step into it more fully. Or, without even thinking about it, we allow ourselves to simply be content with status quo. But when we discover it, we feel as though we have finally come home. And that empowers us in new and profound ways.

One of the reasons living in authenticity and autonomy is so vital is because when we aren't, we are violating our personal design. We are living out of alignment with ourselves. And our minds, spirits, and bodies pay a price for this, including our brains.

Considering that our brain consumes 20 percent of our body's total energy, how important it is to strategically manage our brain energy. And one of the ways to do this is to pay attention to brain adaptation. Our brains, like with our strengths, develop natural preferences—that is, our brains tend to prefer certain functions more than others. When we operate in those functions, our brains expend less energy than when we make choices and take actions outside of our preferred functions.

One of the abilities of the brain is called neuroplasticity—the capacity to adapt by creating new neural networks that get stronger with use. The trick is that there are two kinds of brain adaptations—temporary adapting (desirable; as in, we can learn new things, new behaviors, new skills) and prolonged and excessive adapting (undesirable; as in having to expend unnecessary brain energy that drains us).

My friend Dr. Arlene Taylor, a brain-function expert, uses a simple monetary metaphor to help people understand the impact of prolonged adaptation:

"The differences in energy expenditure may be as great as pennies on the dollar. Expend $1 per second when doing activities that match your innate brain lead. Expend $100 per second when doing activities that draw primarily on a non-preferred cerebral division."[59]

Make sense? In other words, if we continually operate outside the area of our brains' natural preferences, we are burning up energy unnecessarily. And we pay the price for it—we get tired and exhausted more easily, our stress levels increase, we lose our focus, our ability to think clearly and creatively is reduced; if we do this long enough, we become more susceptible to sickness.

Living authentically means making intentional choices to live in alignment with how we are wired—our brain preferences, our strengths, our personalities, our core values. It means embracing all of the unique parts of who we really are, and then leveraging and optimizing them in day-to-day living. This is the strategic way of energy management.

It's not always easy.

Let me illustrate. When listening to the women I work with, I often hear about the pressures they face that most men don't have to face—pressures to conform to cultural expectations that go against who they really are. For example, women are often forced to choose between being liked and being powerful. Whereas men don't have to make this choice—they are actually more liked when they are more powerful.[60]

> If we continually operate outside the area of our brains' natural preferences, we are burning up energy unnecessarily. And we pay the price for it.

Consequently, if women courageously make the choice for decisive and transformational leadership and influence, they pay a price. They're labeled, criticized, judged as being too aggressive, too bitchy, too manly, ice queens, or ballbusters—they've essentially violated the social norms of culture when it comes to gender stereotypes. And many of them as young girls grew up with these messages: "Be quiet! Don't stand out! And by all means, don't be powerful!"

So when some women score high in natural preference in the Influencing category of strengths, I find that they struggle at times with embracing these particular strengths. Influencing strengths like Command, Self-Assurance, Significance, and Competition are often resisted because they aren't seen as strengths for women.

One female manager told me that she had always figured that her Competition strength was a weakness that she needed to work on. She grew up being told it wasn't womanly to beat a man at something. Another female leader made the same observation about her Command strength. "My whole life, I've always been told that this ability for me to be decisive and assertive in rallying people and motivating people with a cause was too strong; it was a weakness I needed to address. 'Dial it back,' I was always told."

So these women were essentially having to make the choice between authenticity, autonomy, and personal power or cultural expectation. This is an unfair and untenable choice. And it is pressuring women to give up their authentic autonomy for the sake of fitting in.

When leaders or peers or organizations have these kinds of unspoken and sometimes spoken biases, they are in reality telling women to not use their brain preferences, their best strengths, to contribute. They're destroying authenticity and forcing them into prolonged and excessive adapting, which causes their brains to burn through energy unnecessarily, making them susceptible to high stress and, ultimately, physical damage. And it disempowers their contributions. Everyone loses.

If we want to motivate people to give their best, to be fully engaged and fully alive in all they do, we have to support individual competency as well as authenticity and autonomy. People need to be given freedom to let their unique voices be heard, to be given a say in what goes on at work and elsewhere, and to perform in their most authentic and competent expression of themselves. These are fundamental human needs. And without them, we assign people to living deteriorating half-lives.

Strategic stops are for the purpose of helping people discover, identify, and learn how to optimize their most authentic and strongest ways of being. Who wouldn't want to live this way?

PERSONAL PAUSES

❚❚ Identify which of the four motivations (Competence, Authenticity, Connectedness, Psychological Safety) ranks highest for you? Lowest? Give illustrations of your ranking.

❚❚ Take the CliftonStrengths assessment (from https://www.gallupstrengthscenter.com/product/en-us/10108/top-5-cliftonstrengths-access?category=assessments). What are your top five strengths? Identify as many ways as you can think of for how each of those five strengths is showing up in your life.

❚❚ Have you ever been told that you are too much or not enough in some way? What did that imply to you? How did it impact you? What did you end up doing about those implied statements?

❚❚ Make a list of the things you are doing that drain your energy (even though you might be good at them). Which are from temporary adapting, and which are from prolonged adapting? With the prolonged adapting actions, how might you be able to stop doing them but find ways to make sure they still get done (in other words, you simply stop doing them or you need to delegate them to someone else to make sure they get done)? Be aware of prolonged brain adaptation taking place in your life and plan a strategy for minimizing those times.

TEAM PAUSES

❚❚ Team sharing question: "What is your number one strength and how are you using it in your personal and professional life?"

❚❚ Are you being asked to contribute your strongest and most energizing abilities to your team? If so, are you stepping in fully? If not, can you ask your manager or leader to let you make those contributions more fully?

❚❚ Team sharing questions: "On a scale of 1–5 (5 being fully, 1 being minimally), which number represents the permission you feel to show up on your team in your authentic self? What specific permission do you need in order to raise that ranking?"

❚❚ Team session evaluation: Is every person being given an opportunity for their voice to heard by everyone else, whatever the conversation is about? Practice going around the circle so that each person can participate and share, instead of using the typical "popcorn" approach (where people just jump in and share, with some always sharing more than others, and others not sharing at all).

Surround Yourself with Support

I was facilitating a team session made up of men. They represented different kinds of expertise, including a mix of managers, directors, and individual contributors. My opening sharing question was, "Tell us your number one strength and share a story of how that strength is showing up for you these days. How are you using it in ways that are meaningful to you?"

The first man to share was one of the directors. He began, "My number one strength is Learner. It means I have a high capacity for curiosity and love the process of learning things. Lately my Learner has been utilized in my personal life for a big reason." His voice broke a bit. "My younger brother was in an accident and is now paralyzed from the neck down."

Everyone on the team showed shock, their eyes opened wide. They all leaned forward as he continued.

"My Learner is really kicking in because I realized that I am now needing to be his primary medical advocate, so I really want to learn everything I can about traumatic brain injury and paralysis."

Tears were beginning to pool in the edges of his eyes. I looked around the circle and saw every man, some with wet eyes, looking intently at him, listening to every word, showing deep empathy.

One of them said, "Wow! I had no idea! I'm so sorry for all of this that you're having to go through. How painful this must be! I'm inspired by your courage and strategic involvement. What can we do to help?"

Several others offered the same kind of caring response.

The sharing continued around the circle. Another man, one of the managers, said, "My number one strength is Empathy—I have a high capacity to feel what others are feeling and use that connection to foster meaningful interaction."

Then he shared, "My wife and I were expecting our second child. We just found out she had a miscarriage." Tears were streaming down his face.

Everyone on the team was leaning in toward him, empathy written all over their faces and expressed in their responses. Many had tears again. The same level of caring had continued.

The sense of meaningful connection among everyone in those moments was palpable. I was in awe, partly because this was a work team and not a social small group, and partly because this was a team of professional men who have stereotypically been labeled by our culture as not willing to share their feelings and emotions with other men.

Interestingly enough, I have seen similar dynamics again and again in my work with teams, and that continues to convict me of the significance and possibility of developing meaningful connectedness and caring among the people we work with.

> Lonelier workers (those who don't feel connected to their colleagues or peers in consequential ways) report lower job satisfaction, fewer promotions, more frequent job switching, and a higher likelihood of quitting their current job in the next six months.

Here's why facilitating more meaningful social connections in the workplace is so vital. Research shows that lonelier workers (those who don't feel connected to their colleagues or peers in consequential ways) report lower job satisfaction, fewer promotions, more frequent job switching, and a higher likelihood of quitting their current job in the next six months. Feeling a lack of workplace social support is associated with similar negative business outcomes—these negative impacts, for example, are costing the United Kingdom alone upward of $3.5 billion every year.[61] Organizations are paying a heavy price for social disconnection among their employees.

What's more, as the last chapter emphasized, for people to be fully motivated to do and be their best in whatever setting they're in—to feel fully alive and engaged—they need four elements in their lives: competency, authenticity, connectedness, and psychological safety. I addressed the first two in the last chapter. Let's look at the third human motivator.

THE FOUR FACTORS OF INNOVATIVE ENGAGEMENT

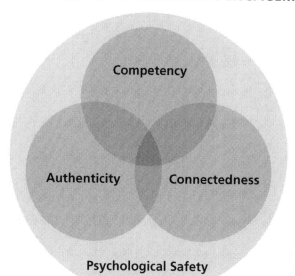

3. Developing Connectedness

This third human motivation is a vital mission if you want to motivate and empower the people in your organization to perform at their highest potential. At our most basic level, human beings hunger for meaningful connection with others. This is one of the driving forces of our evolution as a species in our work as well as our outside-work lives.

That's what I witnessed as I held the space for the team of men in the previous story. When given the space and opportunity, they became very honest and vulnerable with each other. And the outcome was a deepening of their relationships, along with the ability to work more effectively together.

Amy C. Edmondson, who is the Novartis professor of Leadership and Management at Harvard Business School and has spent the last 20 years studying about what makes organizations successful, articulates a keen observation about what's necessary in today's increasingly global and complex companies. For knowledge work to succeed, she explains, "the workplace must be one where people feel able to share their knowledge. This means sharing concerns, questions, mistakes, and half-formed ideas … Today's employees, at all levels, spend 50% more time collaborating than they did 20 years ago."[62]

This suggests a very significant implication. As she emphasizes, "Hiring talented individuals is not enough. They have to be able to work well together."[63]

People skills are fast becoming the most important skill for success in the workplace—the ability to make and sustain meaningful connections with others in a way that builds up the people on the team instead of tearing them down.

So what does this look like in the workplace? What kind of connectedness is most valuable and how is it achieved?

My wife, Shasta, is a professional speaker, renowned friendship/relationship expert, and author of two books on the topic. She makes the following observation about what it takes to deepen the social connections we have. She calls it the Frientimacy Triangle.[64] There are three requirements for meaningful connections: positivity, consistency, and vulnerability. Every meaningful relationship needs all three elements in varying degrees, depending on how shallow or deep you want the relationship to be.

She summarizes each piece of the triangle like this:

1. **Positivity basically means positive feelings.**
   Positivity is the result we feel in healthy relationships as we are left feeling good from such things as pride, awe, empathy, kindness, acts of service, gratitude, laughter, and affirmation. Friendship is absolutely about two people raising the emotional happiness of each other.

2. **Consistency basically means consistent interaction.**
   Consistency is where we log the hours and devote the time to each other; it's how we build a shared history and make memories; it's the repetition or regularity that develops patterns, rituals, and expectations in our relationship.

3. **Vulnerability basically means safe sharing.**
   Vulnerability is the sharing and revealing of who we are; it's two people choosing to get to know each other; it's allowing someone else to hear our ideas, know our opinions, validate our feelings, and listen to our experiences. Vulnerability is what leads to us ultimately feeling seen and known by another, which is required for feeling loved or respected.

Like a formula, a healthy relationship must have all three: consistency, positivity, and vulnerability. They are all required; take one out and we don't have a healthy friendship.

So imagine the advantage a person has in the workplace, the environment so many of us spend the most amount of time in. We enjoy built-in consistency. And if we work in a team with others, this consistency is an everyday experience. The more consistency we log, the more we are able to build trust with each other.

And then, when we add positivity and vulnerability—we actually enjoy being with each other because our people are fundamentally positive and everyone is willing to be open, honest, and appropriately vulnerable with each other—we can actually build positive and meaningful connections. And these connections build enjoyable depth over time.

Notice in my story of the team of men how these three requirements were central to their experience in that session. They were fundamentally positive—they laughed with each other, they each felt seen and heard, and they left the session feeling good about each other and themselves. They were enjoying a regular consistency being on the leadership team. They had the advantage of logging many hours together. Their trust levels were quite high. And as a result, they were willing to be deeply honest and vulnerable with each other.

4. Psychological Safety

Google has done the most comprehensive study about high-performing teams and what makes them so successful. It's a great illustration of the Frientimacy Triangle at work. They called the study Project Aristotle. Pulling together experts from psychology, organizational psychology, sociology, anthropology, and business management, along with engineers and researchers, Google tasked them with finding what sets their most successful teams apart from the others.

Their primary conclusion is profoundly simple. The highest-performing teams intentionally develop a climate they called "psychological safety."

"There's a team culture in which the team is safe for interpersonal risk-taking. So psychological safety is a sense of confidence that the team will not embarrass, reject or punish someone for speaking up. It describes a team climate characterized by interpersonal trust and mutual respect in which people are comfortable being themselves."[65]

The researchers discovered that what distinguishes the highly effective teams from the dysfunctional or even average teams is how the team members treat each other. The great teams show respect, honor, empathy, and mutual support.

Three of the ways those attitudes are revealed are by everyone having equal participation and speaking time; by everyone being able to understand each other, including recognizing the nonverbal cues (like facial expressions, tone of voice, and body language) of how people are feeling and what they are thinking; and by everyone being willing to share personal stories, to be vulnerable with each other, and to build a more meaningful connection with each other.[66]

> What distinguishes the highly effective teams from the dysfunctional or even average teams is how the team members treat each other. The great teams show respect, honor, empathy, and mutual support.

What I've learned working with hundreds of leaders and teams is that this kind of climate doesn't just happen spontaneously. It is developed through great intentionality, especially by leaders. Leaders set the tone by their personal modeling and the shared expectations they generate. And then it happens because everyone is willing to show up with and for each other in authentic and honest ways.

This is why, during team sessions, I always use sharing questions that involve personal stories, whether from work or from the rest of life. When we share personal stories, it establishes an opportunity for us to create bridges and connections with each other. It raises the possibility for feeling empathy for others. When we feel empathy, we have more trust and more confidence and more respect for each other. And the mutual support level increases exponentially.

That's why all the research shows that in this kind of environment, innovation happens in the most generative way possible. The best ideas emerge when there is no judgment for sharing. And then those are the ideas that get acted upon.

Having a team climate that encourages connectedness matters.

"What Project Aristotle has taught people within Google is that no one wants to put on a 'work face' when they get to the office. No one wants to leave part of their personality and inner life at home. But to be fully present at work, to feel 'psychologically safe,' we must know that we can be free enough, sometimes, to share the things that scare us without fear of recriminations. We must be able to talk about what is messy or sad, to have hard conversations with colleagues who are driving us crazy. We can't be focused just on efficiency. Rather, when we start the morning by collaborating with a team of engineers and then send emails to our marketing colleagues and then jump on a conference call, we want to know that those people really hear us. We want to know that work is more than just labor."[67]

What is so impressive and significant about Dr. Edmondson's and Google's research is that it shows how vital establishing a culture of meaningful connectedness is in today's workplace. And Shasta Nelson's picture of the three requirements of meaningful connections provides the vital framework for how to create this culture.

Not only do human beings have a fundamental need to belong, we also need a safe space in which to belong. Our sense of belonging requires being seen and valued for who we are and what we contribute. We hunger for mutual conversation, empathy, respect, and basic kindness. We want to feel supported and validated in a positive atmosphere of mutual encouragement rather than judgment and criticism.

This doesn't mean that we can't disagree with each other or call each other to accountability or confront when necessary. But it means that all of this is done in a climate of mutual support, encouragement, and validation. You have to feel this. And so do the people who work with you.

Do you work in that kind of culture? Do you feel that your need for connectedness is being adequately met? How would you evaluate your relationships based upon the three requirements of healthy connections?

> Not only do human beings have a fundamental need to belong, we also need a safe space in which to belong. Our sense of belonging requires being seen and valued for who we are and what we contribute.

If we're going to bring back more humanity to the workplace, then we have to provide more effective opportunities for people to connect in meaningful ways with each other in both teams and in the whole workplace. We have to be willing to create a psychologically safe environment in which people can be themselves, be seen, be known more fully, and be invited to contribute their very best.

What would it take for you to create this kind of social and relational climate with the people you work with and the people you live with?

I was facilitating a group conversation with a congregation that was beginning the process of putting together a strategic plan for their mission and vision. We had just finished a SWOT analysis—an activity designed to bring clarity and focus to people's understanding of their organization's strengths, weaknesses, opportunities, and threats. Everyone had put up on the wall 2–3 sticky notes of suggestions for each of those categories.

As I debriefed the experience with the participants, I asked them what it felt like going through this process. One by one, people stood up and commented about how empowering it felt. One couple stood up and, with deep emotion, said, "This is the first time we have felt seen and heard in this group. We've always felt a bit on the outside and different from everyone else. Our interests and passions have never really been tapped here. Today, we have felt we were given a voice and that our voices really matter to everyone."

On the one hand, it was tragic that this couple had felt so isolated and undervalued in their congregation for so many years. As a result, the group had never received this couple's ideas, wisdom, and best contributions.

But on the other hand, better late than never. Because a safe space had been created for the whole group, and because the opportunity was given for everyone to express their views and feelings, this couple was able to be vulnerable and communicate their need and interests. And the group responded positively. What's more, the specific ideas this couple had suggested in the SWOT activity turned out to be hugely strategic and visionary. The group ended up adopting their suggestions, resulting in an innovative outcome and more meaningful engagement for the couple.

> Meaningful social connectedness matters in the process of working together.

Team and group climate matter. Meaningful social connectedness matters in the process of working together. This atmosphere doesn't happen spontaneously, appearing out of thin air. It must be fostered and encouraged by leaders and team members because they believe in it and deeply desire it for everyone. People need to become more aware of the three non-negotiables of healthy relationships and how to provide all three on their teams and in their organizations.

Imagine having this kind of climate in a family, where every person's voice is important and is asked for—whether from children or parents; where it's a psychologically safe place to express feelings, ideas, hopes, and dreams without the fear of recrimination, judgment, criticism, or disregard; where every person is given the appropriate amount of agency and freedom to be themselves; where, in the midst of all this diversity, there exists a spirit of love, compassionate accountability, empathy, respect, understanding, and meaningful connectedness.

Whether you are a leader in an organization, a parent to children, or a part of any tribe or group, it is within your grasp to pay attention to these four human motivations—competency, authenticity, connectedness, and psychological safety. You can choose to show up in those environments as a transformational force for belonging and meaningful relationships.

When this happens, we can see each other in new and empowering ways and act with more compassion and kindness.

One of my favorite stories that Stephen Covey tells in his book *The 7 Habits of Highly Effective People*[68] is about a time when he was riding the subway in New York City after a consulting gig in downtown Manhattan. As usual, everyone sitting and standing around him was absorbed in their own personal world—reading the newspaper or a book, listening to music with earbuds, sleeping or meditating with eyes closed—everyone was completely zoned out.

Until, at one of the stops, a father and his two young children got into Covey's train car. The father immediately sat down and closed his eyes. His kids, however, began making a bigger-than-life commotion. They were shouting, running around, running into people, knocking newspapers out of people's hands, pulling out earbuds from ears—in general, acting like demon-children.

Covey watched and felt his blood pressure rising with every heartbeat. He was clearly getting angry, not just with these unruly children, but especially with the father, who was refusing to corral them.

"Come on, man!" Covey said to himself. "Can't you see your kids are destroying this car? Do something!"

The father seemed completely oblivious. He remained silent with his eyes closed.

Finally Covey had had enough. He got up, stormed over to the father, and rather firmly tapped him on the shoulder. "Excuse me, sir," he said loudly.

The father opened his eyes as though coming out of a daze, glanced around him, and then looked up at Covey standing rather menacingly above him.

"Sir, your children are completely wild. They're disrupting everyone in this car. Can't you please control them?"

The father looked over and, for the first time, noticed his kids. Then he looked back up at Covey. "Oh, I guess you're right. I should do something about it. We just came from the hospital where their mother died about an hour ago. I don't know what to think. And I guess they don't know how to handle it either."

At that moment, Covey writes, he experienced a paradigm shift. He had been deeply angry with this man, making big judgments about him as a parent. And then he received new information. It changed everything for him.

He said, because I saw differently, I thought differently, I felt differently, and so I acted differently.

His irritation gone, placing his hand on the grieving father's shoulder, he said, "Oh, I'm so sorry, sir! So sorry about your loss! Is there anything I can do for you?"

This is the power of seeing each other in transparent ways. When we see each other for who we really are, in more of the context of our lives, we build deeper connections. Our empathy gets tapped. Our sense of belonging is stimulated. And we are empowered to act in more caring and supportive ways.

The good news is that it is never too late to pay more attention to the climate in our groups. When we do, we can change our important environments for the good with remarkable and transformational outcomes.

The world desperately needs more strategic stops carved out for these life-enhancing purposes.

PERSONAL PAUSES

▣ On a scale of 1–10 (1 being never, 10 being always), which number represents your typical experience at home and at work of feeling safe and seen? Give examples.

▣ Make a list of what you need the most in your interactions with others to feel safe and seen. What needs to happen with you and with others to raise the above number?

▣ Name people in your life that you feel highly supported by— you have a high level of trust in them. And you can go to them (or talk to them any time) knowing you will be heard and supported. Who in your life might you invite to be someone like that to you?

▣ What specific behaviors can you exhibit more of to be a safe, supportive, and trusted person other people?

TEAM PAUSES

❚❚ Team sharing questions: "On a scale of 1–5 (1 being not safe, 5 being very safe), which number represents your feeling of psychological safety on your team? What would it take from yourself or from others to raise that number for you?"

❚❚ Team sharing question: "Rank the three requirements for healthy relationships (positivity, consistency, vulnerability) in the order in which you experience each element in your team interactions (1 being the most experienced, 3 the least experienced)."

❚❚ Team sharing question: "Share 1–2 specific ways (behaviors, attitudes) you can help increase your and everyone's experience of each of the three requirements."

❚❚ Plan a social event for just your team, making sure you have intentional activities at that event that increase positivity, consistency (in this case trust), and vulnerability. This should include some sharing questions, fun experiences (like games, activities, eating, or refreshments), and meaningful interactions (like getting to know each other beyond just work roles—hobbies, unique life experiences, some joys and sad moments). This is about shaping more meaningful connections with each other.

Sabbath Your Time

The San Juan Islands are one of my favorite sailing locations in the world. They are a stunningly beautiful archipelago of 400 islands and rocks off the northern coast of Washington State. The anchorages, small villages and towns, island landscapes, and abundant wildlife are exquisitely beautiful. I've sailed there for 30 years.

On one of our trips, when my kids were small, we were sailing in the large channel between two of the bigger islands. The winds were heavy, and my small 25-foot MacGregor was being pushed to its limits. It was actually quite exhilarating as we sped over the water, heeled way over, with me fighting the tiller as best I could to keep the boat on tack.

Dark clouds started forming in the sky. I looked around the large channel to see what other boats were doing (sailors always check out other boats to measure progress as well as direction and to notice their strategies). They still had their sails up—most of them, at least. I felt confident. So we kept sailing and enjoying the ride.

I noticed the wind picking up in force and velocity. White caps were starting to form on the waves. I looked up at our mainsail. I had it close-hauled, and it was full and tight. But soon, because the wind was getting stronger, it was beginning to flap. Not a good sign.

I looked around again at the other boats. Some of them had dropped their mainsails. "Interesting sign," I thought to myself. "But this is so much fun. Why stop now? Let me just keep this tack going as long as I can. This speed is great!"

Suddenly we heard a loud clap of thunder. That got my attention. And then the sky opened up and spit out a torrential mouthful of rain. That kept my attention. I looked around and saw that all the boats had dropped their sails and were motoring to safety. That mobilized my full attention.

So in the midst of very strong winds and a literal downpour of rain, I pull-started the 7.5 horsepower Honda outboard motor. It started with an uncharacteristic two pulls. Phew! I rushed as quickly as possible to drop the mainsail and tie it up. Furling the headsail, I looked around to spot the closest harbor or cove. Not too far away was a small bay, so I immediately steered straight there.

My kids were pretty scared by this time. A full-on storm was whipping all over us. I was feeling a bit faint-hearted too (understatement of the year). "Hurry, hurry, little engine!" I was willing it and pleading by this time. "Get us into that bay!"

Our little sailboat chugged into the small cove. It was fairly well-protected by the three sides of the island. The wind was still out there. Rain was pouring down. But the waters were calmer and survivable in the cove. It's hard to describe the feeling of relief. We spent several hours waiting out the storm in the safety of that bay.

One of the important things I've learned through the sailing years of my life is that when the winds blow with gale force, finding a safe harbor is extremely helpful to one's quality of life.

Sailors know you can't control the wind. You can't tell it to stop, lessen its force, or blow harder. You can't create the wind. You can only leverage it, optimize it, and utilize it for your benefit to get to where you want to go. Or you protect yourself from it by waiting it out in as safe a place as you can find.

So what does this look like in the rest of life? What kind of strategic stop could create a safe harbor in the midst of the winds that blow all around us?

Finding Your Island of Stillness: What Should It Look Like?

We live in a world that is filled with the shocks of life—stress, anxiety, fear, danger, catastrophes, violence, failure, guilt, shame, hurt, pain, brokenness. The list is long. We're surrounded by forces that drain us, damage our dignity, and call into question our identity and sense of worth.

In organizations, we live in a world that is filled with disruption, change, loss of control, failure, difficult coworkers, hard-to-please managers, fluctuating stock valuations, product duds, displeased stakeholders, never-ending meetings. The list is long here, too. We're surrounded by forces that drain us, damage our dignity, and call into question our identity and sense of worth.

Each year seems to bring with it a faster and faster pace of life, more demands on us, and more things to do to just keep up and survive—not to mention what it takes to go beyond maintenance to what often seems like the lofty, luxurious dream of actually thriving.

There is so much of our humanity that is getting lost in our obsessions with busyness and productivity. We desperately need regular safe harbors, a secure point of reference in the middle of the rat race, a sanctuary in time in which we can stop and regroup, be refreshed and reassured, and reground ourselves in what it means to be truly human and alive.

So what would that kind of strategic stop look like?

The respected Jewish philosopher and theologian Abraham Heschel described one such powerful reference point. He called it Sabbath. Here's the way he described the concept and experience:

"In the tempestuous ocean of time and toil there are islands of stillness where man may enter a harbor and reclaim his dignity. The island is the Sabbath, a day of detachment from things, instruments and practical affairs, as well as attachment to the spirit ... The Sabbath is the exodus from tension, the liberation of man from his own muddiness, the installation of man as a sovereign in the world of time."[69]

The following are seven guideposts to help inform your process of carving out intentional space to breathe more soul into your personal and professional life. They are based upon the seven phrases that make up Heschel's quotation, helping you chart your way forward to being more intentional about sabbathing your weekly time.

The goal for this process is to begin shaping a practice of sabbath in your life rhythm—the discipline of stopping, moving past the normal distractions, centering yourself on what's most important, and connecting with your inner wisdom, allowing more soul depth to be breathed into your busy life.

This is about developing the art of leveraging the blowing winds in your life. Trimming your sails. Being nimble in your tack (your direction) while focusing on your destination. Learning how to navigate the changing conditions of your life in a way that keeps your identity, purpose, and character intact. Where you learn the joy of thriving, not just surviving, no matter your external environment and conditions. It's about finding your most authentic, empowering reference point and choosing to return to it in the regular rhythm of your life.

So here are the seven guideposts for you.

1. "In the tempestuous ocean of time and toil ..."

Where in your life do you most feel like a "tempestuous ocean"? Where do you feel battered around by the wind and the waves?

What is it about your "time and toil" (time, work, and relationships) that makes you at times feel out of control, powerless, overburdened, or sometimes even purposeless or directionless? What internal and external pressures are you feeling? How are you dealing with them?

> Where in your life do you most feel like a "tempestuous ocean"? Where do you feel battered around by the wind and the waves?

We live in a global culture that puts such an unforgiving priority on productivity and accomplishment that the amount of pressure we often feel is relentless. None of us is immune.

In Japan, where the burden to put in long work hours as a sign of loyalty to the company is deeply ingrained, thousands of people die every year from heart attacks, strokes, and other conditions, including suicide. The government's Labor Standards Office reports this as being brought on by spending too much time at work.

Miwa Sado, 31 years old, who worked at the country's public broadcasting station headquarters in Tokyo, logged 159 hours of overtime and took only two days off in the month leading up to her death from heart failure in July 2013. The government office investigating her death attributed it to, as the Japanese call it, *karoshi* (death by overwork).

Another individual committed suicide on Christmas Day after having put in over 100 hours of overtime during the month before. The authorities labeled the cause of death *karoshi*, as well. The person had posted on social media shortly before death, "I want to die. I'm physically and mentally shattered."[70]

No culture is completely immune from this "tempestuous ocean of time and toil." It might not be from work-related pressure. It might also be from relational pressures, emotional triggers, a generalized feeling of a deep lack of aliveness, or spiritual dis-ease. And our bodies, minds, and hearts are paying the price.

My wife, Shasta, and I will often share with each other at the end of a busy work week about where in our bodies we're feeling drained of energy. We ask, "How does that lack of energy show up in your emotional, relational, physical, and spiritual parts? What specifically are you noticing right now?"

It's quite amazing how much impact day-to-day life during the week has on the various parts of our lives. And we're learning how to identify that specifically enough so that we can strategically shape our sabbathing during the weekend—in other words, so we can know what kind of sabbath experience we most need in order to refocus, reground, and re-center ourselves effectively.

Where are you feeling battered around by the winds and waves of your life existence? What is the tempest that is creating this for you? Is there something proactive you are doing to deal with this?

2. "There are islands of stillness where man may enter a harbor and reclaim his dignity."

Picture yourself in an island harbor of stillness after having been buffeted by heavy wind and waves out in the open seas. What does it look like to you? What does it feel like?

I can tell you, as my opening sailing story in this chapter described, my anxiety level and the corresponding adrenaline production in my whole body were reacting feverishly to being caught in open water in the middle of a furious storm. Talk about fight or flight. In this case, I had to do everything within my power to leverage the fight side of that equation. My safety simply could not afford only the flight option. I had to engage both responses.

When we got into that safe harbor created by a protected bay, there was a relief hard to describe in words. Little by little my adrenaline production lowered and dissipated. My heartbeat went down, my perspiring palms dried, my dilated pupils returned to normal. The cortisol rushing through my system was draining away. There is nothing like the power of calm.

Though we still could hear the boom of the thunder in the distance, it was mostly the pattering of the rain on the boat we heard as we huddled inside.

Stillness. What does that feel like to you? What gives you that experience and feeling?

Is it feeling safe? Does it produce a kind of inner calm? Is it feeling grounded and secure on a stable foundation? Is it feeling provided for so you don't have to worry and be anxious? Is it feeling that you're enough just as you are without the pressure to be something more in order to be accepted in your relationships, whether at work or home?

Islands of stillness. More necessary these days than ever with so much chaos all around us in this world.

Notice what Heschel describes as an outcome of entering the harbor in the island of stillness. We reclaim our dignity.

Dignity. What a powerful word.

All of the commotion and chaos, arguments, conflict, violence, hate, and destructive diminishing of humanity are inflicting a massive toll on human dignity in today's culture. Respect, honor, and empathy for self, much less for others, is at an all-time low. Just read the stories in the daily news or go on Facebook and scroll through the news feed filled with vitriol, hate, and disrespect. I hear evidences of this toll all the time from my clients.

Truth is, diminished dignity produces destructive people.

> Truth is, diminished dignity produces destructive people.

What does dignity mean to you? What does dignity feel like? Where have you perhaps lost your sense of dignity? What happens at times to take your dignity?

Significantly enough, what often destroys our personal dignity are our own limiting beliefs that manifest in our self-talk. When certain things happen to us, we disparage ourselves in ways that we would never do publicly to other people. We say things like, "I'm so stupid!" "I'm such a loser!" "I don't deserve this [something really good that comes to you]!"

I've been around a lot of religious people who have a built-in theology about God that depicts themselves as unworthy and only God as worthy. They use God to do two things: disparage themselves and elevate God. It's always a binary choice—either/or. "I'm not worthy of anything good. But thank God that God is good!" I'm bad. But God is good.

Whatever your world view, this kind of binary view that evidences itself in our self-talk is hugely damaging to human dignity. Consequently, there are a lot of us who are walking around with damaged spirits—our self-esteem in tatters, our sense of unworthiness like a hurricane wind shattering our souls, destroying our essential humanity.

Again, diminished dignity produces destructive people.

Picture yourself regaining a sense of dignity. What does that feel like? When do you most feel dignity in your life? What kind of self-talk do you hear when you feel dignity?

Whatever kind of practice you develop for your island of stillness, it must include a renewed sense of self. It has to involve practices that empower you to reclaim your dignity in a world that continues to try to rob you of it. You have to practice grounding yourself in the truth of who you really are.

Imagine taking a day every week (as Heschel is describing) in an island of stillness that serves as a refuge from the battering we often feel in our culture. Imagine a specifically shaped recovery time to reconnect with our truest selves and the truest selves of the most important others in our lives. A day to reclaim personal and relational dignity.

3. "The island is the Sabbath, a day of detachment from things, instruments and practical affairs ..."

The Hebrew word *sabbath* literally means to stop, cease from, rest. I like my words *strategic stop*. Sabbath isn't simply stopping for stopping's sake. It's stopping for a strategic goal. I'll talk about the history of this practice a bit later because it provides some powerful motivations and goals for us.

But for now, Heschel points out that this island in time called Sabbath is for the purpose of detachment in order to attach to something of higher value. Detachment is a significant practice. This letting go of something is what opens up space to receive something else.

Consider how locals in various parts of the world have trapped monkeys. They take a gourd, drill a small hole in one end just large enough for the monkey's hand, and then place a treat or some food at the bottom. The monkey, wanting the treat, puts its hand into the gourd and grabs the desired prize. But as long as its hand grasps the treat, it cannot pull the hand out through the small hole. It's stuck. And it ends up losing its freedom.

In spite of our impressive human capacity for high-level reasoning, we often default to a stance of grabbing and refusing to let go. We don't realize that we're giving up our freedom in exchange for what we're desperately hanging on to because we think we need it.

We hold on to grudges. Past hurts. Unforgiveness. Judgments against others. Destructive biases. Limiting beliefs. Negative self-talk. Anxieties. Status quo. Tradition. Fear of change. Outdated ideas. Damaging relationships. Consumerism around material possessions we let define us. Wobbly stilts we think are propping up our identity. Our need to control. Image. Busyness.

Detachment is what opens up space to receive something far better and more sustainable.

We have grabbed ahold of these things we think are treasures that we simply have to possess. But at the same time, we have been tricked into giving up our freedom.

> Detachment is what opens up space to receive something far better and more sustainable.

Sabbath as an island of stillness that comes every seven days is a strategic stop to provide us perspective. The long view. Evaluation opportunity. Reflection about what is holding us back from our full potential as human beings. It's a tool to reclaim honesty. To open up our tightly fisted hold on the things, instruments, and practical affairs we're allowing to define us.

Imagine carving out a weekly day that provides you opportunity to refocus, recenter, realign yourself with what you hold most dear, with your deepest core values. And in order to do that, you are invited to let go of that which keeps you from being free to do just that—like taking a technology sabbath, or consumer sabbath, or productivity sabbath—a day to simply step into becoming human beings again after a busy week, in order to attach to what is ultimately most valuable and the deepest part of ourselves: our human spirit.

4. "… as well as attachment to the spirit."

We detach from all the things in our lives we are convinced define us and provide us our worth. We do this in order to attach to the truest parts of our selves. We take this time to reclaim those pieces of us that we neglect or lose during the hubbub of the busy week—the parts that we misguidedly exchange for what we think is more vital to our survival. After a week of intense doing, we stop to reattach to our being. And it is in this reattachment, this reclamation, that we find our deepest peace and stillness. We are re-energized with renewed courage, confidence, and hope.

So what do you need to detach from right now to have stillness in your spirit, heart, mind, and body? What are the things, instruments, and practical affairs you might be allowing to define you? What do you need to let go of right now to feel totally free?

What does it feel like to stop from the rat race? How would it feel to do this regularly? How could you establish a sabbath as a regular practice?

Heschel describes Sabbath as a day for engaging in this powerful personal and relational practice. Imagine that. Possessing an island of stillness for 24 hours because you've chosen to anchor in a safe harbor. What would that look like for you?

There's an ancient scripture that says, "Be still and know that I am God." Whatever your view of the divine, whatever your worldview, what this is suggesting is that your most deeply human grounding is accessed most productively in the midst of stillness, quietness, and calm. There's a reason we are called human beings instead of human doings.

To use nautical terminology, taking a sabbath is like dropping anchor and calming your boat in stillness, securing it from the buffeting of the tides, currents, and winds. In this safe zone, you are reminded of who you are and what brings you the most joy and peace. You are empowered with greater courage and confidence so that when you sail back out to the open seas, facing all the elements again, you can do it even more strategically, confidently, and effectively.

> Your most deeply human grounding is accessed most productively in the midst of stillness, quietness, and calm. There's a reason we are called human beings instead of human doings.

Reattaching to the spirit of life infuses your own spirit with a larger trust in the flow of life. It's attaching to a collective spirit of humanity and all that is good with the human race. Every day we have painful reminders that there is pain and suffering and evil in the world. We are tempted to forget that there is also good; that there are people all over the world who are living out of compassion, grace, forgiveness, and hope; working tirelessly on behalf of those who are disadvantaged, disempowered, and distressed. We forget this truth so often, and so we are tempted to live with a kind of despair, hopelessness, and powerlessness.

But when every sabbath arrives, we are attaching to the spirit; we are stepping back into the powerful flow of love that runs all over the world. We are encouraged to trust in that flow, to participate in that flow, to see that there is more than simply our individual existence; there is a global family, the powerful spirit of humanity, working for the good of all. We are not alone. And for those of us who believe in a compassionate God, we are reminded that God is in control and moving the world with this flow of love—and love is the most powerful force in the world. It's an unstoppable river with infinite power to transform, like the waters that carved out the Grand Canyon.

Attaching to this spirit instills hope within us. And hope is what drives our confidence and ability to face life with agency and the power of positive transformation.

Heschel now reiterates this perspective by describing three wonderful final outcomes.

5. "The Sabbath is the exodus from tension …"

His reference to Jewish history here is significant. The Exodus was the Jews' deliverance from slavery in the land of Egypt. Enslaved in bondage for over 400 years, the Hebrew people were entrenched in a foreign country, forced into hard labor building bricks for the pharaohs' monuments to superiority. Little by little their personal and national identities were draining away. With every attack of their slave masters' whips on their backs, they were reminded that they were not free. They were slaves who existed only for the purpose of producing monuments to pharaoh. They were nothing more than human doings.

Have you heard the story of the biblical Exodus, when waters of the Red Sea parted to provide the Israelites escape from Egypt and the pursuing armies of the pharaoh? Actually, that was not the only exodus that liberated them. As Heschel is reminding us, every seventh day the Hebrews were allowed their Sabbath—their exodus from the tensions and sufferings of the week. A day of liberation to be reminded of their true identity. "We are not slaves. We are free. God's children. With a destiny for ultimate freedom in our own Promised Land."

For 24 hours, these enslaved Hebrews engaged in practices and rituals to remind themselves of their ultimate value and purpose. "You may be able to take our bodies and use them for six days. But the seventh day reminds us that no one can take our spirit. Inside, we are truly free!"

The tension that comes from feeling overwhelmed in our daily lives—stressed by all the expectations dumped on our shoulders, anxious from all the chaos and uncertainty around us, beholden to employers or stakeholders or others who remind us that we're working for them, not vice versa—takes a toll on our psyches and bodies. We are tempted to see our value as nothing more than human doings.

Truth is, this tension kills. Live with it unabated long enough and we collapse under the strain.

But the gift of sabbath can restore our humanity like it did for the ancient Hebrews. It can return us to human beings.

As I write this, I'm listening to Aaron Copeland's "Fanfare for the Common Man." It's one of the most powerful and inspiring pieces of music to me. Exclusively for brass and percussion, the bold chords strike a stunningly majestic and triumphant sound. It's as though the composer is trying to tell us that there is tremendous power in being the common man. Though common, we are not ordinary. We are powerful and triumphant, with inestimable value. The storms may crash around us, the gale-force winds blow on us, but we have an island of stillness where we can be anchored in our truth. There is more than what we see and feel all around us. We are bound together by our common humanity. We are not alone.

While listening to this piece, I got a text from my wife sharing the news that one of our friends just received. Her husband has been diagnosed with a brain tumor. She and her daughter have been sobbing for a whole day, afraid, uncertain, feeling lost in this news. My heart aches for them.

In a world filled with pain, suffering, and overwhelm—when the hurricane winds slam into our lives, threatening to capsize us—we need islands of stillness, places and times when we can be liberated from our tensions and be enfolded by the supportive embrace of people who believe in us as we are, not as others think we should be; people who will remind us of who we are and what we're capable of; people who can walk with us through the darkness, helping us in our exodus from the tension of bondage into the hope of liberation and freedom.

Imagine those ancient Jews coming to the Sabbath and being embraced by each other, binding up each other's wounds and bruises from the slave

> In a world filled with pain, suffering, and overwhelm—when the hurricane winds slam into our lives, threatening to capsize us—we need islands of stillness.

masters, anointing each other's broken bodies, reminding each other of their true identity and destiny. In community, they experienced the inner liberation of a future promised land of freedom.

Imagine carving this kind of dedicated and balm-filled time into your weekly rhythm.

6. "... the liberation of man from his own muddiness ..."

Heschel uses an interesting word choice: *muddiness*. What does it mean in this context? What has gotten muddy?

Within the narrative of the Jews' slavery in Egypt, six days a week, grunting and groaning under the weight of the heavy bricks and stones forced onto their backs, they were constantly tempted to forget their true identity. After endless years of this backbreaking work, their view of themselves and their destiny got muddy. Can you blame them? They were being told every day that their only value and worth were in how much they produced for the pharaoh and the empire. They were nothing more than human doings, doing the bidding of someone else without the luxury of refusal or question.

Sound familiar?

Think of all the forces around us that try to define us and our value. We're being labeled all the time.

And there's another kind of muddiness that confuses our sense of life. It's not just about identity. It's also about worth and value.

According to some estimates, every day you and I are bombarded by anywhere between 4,000 and 10,000 advertisements and marketing messages, all competing for our attention. From the moment we wake up to the moment we collapse in bed, we are inundated with a tsunami of messages essentially beckoning for our consideration and devotion. The underlying implication is that we simply are not enough the way we are—to be more complete, we need what they are offering.

This has shaped our culture to build itself on consumerism and consumption. We are only as good or valuable or worthy as our last purchase. It's often incredibly subtle, and often blatant. And yet marketing continues because it works. We buy into it. Everyone else does, so the pressure is on us to keep up.

Our sense of value and worth becomes tied to what we have in our homes, offices, bank accounts, and on our properties. Our sense of contentment or happiness is tied to consuming, whether stuff or experiences. And the comparison game keeps us pushing for more and more.

When you see a neighbor drive into their driveway with a brand new car, how does it make you feel? When you see a friend post pictures on Facebook of their latest exotic getaway, how does it make you feel? When you hear about your work peer getting a promotion, how do you feel? When one of your parent-friends brags to you that their child just received a full merit scholarship to Harvard, how do you feel? Happy and content for them? Or a bit jealous and dissatisfied with your life? It's a tough game.

Our day-to-day culture presses us into a fundamental muddiness about where our value, worth, and contentment come from. And when we stop and reflect about it, we realize that we're living under a heavy burden of expectation and desire. We've become human doings, doing what the world around us is shouting for us to do in order to feel a sense of value and worth, in order to be somebody of significance. We feel keenly our lack. And soon we've bought into the fantasy that we are not enough as we are—we need more.

Muddiness.

Imagine the Hebrews mixing the mud every day in order to build bricks for the pharaoh. That mud painfully represents slavery, a co-opting of their true destiny for a subhuman existence. And yet that same mud also reflects back to them their origin story as humans. That moment in creation when God took the mud of the earth, shaped it into a human form, and then breathed life into it, forever shaping human destiny as sovereigns in the world with eternal value and worth.

This is true for us, as well. Even in the midst of the muddiness of our lives, when we're tempted to narrow our vision of self and life into a subhuman existence, we are invited to change the way we see it—as a reflection of our profound human destiny.

Into this muddy swamp comes a radical gift. Heschel called it the Sabbath. A tool to drain the swamp of individual and community expectations. Every seven days, 24 hours are set aside to remember, to be reminded, to be refreshed and revitalized by the truth about our identity, value, and worth. A day of liberation from our muddiness, confusion, and sometimes misplaced priorities. An opportunity for a reset before a new week is begun.

For this to work, we must be willing to establish not just a stop-doing list but also a new kind of to-do list—ways to help remind us of our truth and what really matters most.

7. "... the installation of man as a sovereign in the world of time."

How would you describe your relationship to time? Do you ever feel like it controls you, that you're too often a victim of time because of forces beyond your control, that there's a scarcity of time to do the things you really want to do?

Notice the phrases we often use to describe this relationship: "I just don't have the time"; "I'm sorry, I'm too busy"; "We've run out of time"; "I feel so rushed"; "It feels like time is standing still"; "Wow, time sure flies"; "Where has the time gone?"; "The time is dragging by"; "I feel pressured by the time"; "You only have so much time to do the things you need and want to do"; "Time doesn't grow on trees"; "You have too much time on your hands"; "I feel like I'm rushing to catch up"; "I'm running out of time."

It often feels like we have a kind of bipolar relationship to time: we're either rushing to catch up or bored out of our minds. Here's the way Dr. Gay Hendricks puts it:

"Think of how many times in your life you've heard someone say, 'I have exactly the right amount of time to enjoy everything I'm doing.' I don't believe I've ever heard anybody say anything like that. Most people seem to live at the two extremes of the time continuum: rushing to stay ahead of the clock because they're busy, or virtually brain-dead with boredom because they don't have enough to do."[71]

> It often feels like we have a kind of bipolar relationship to time: we're either rushing to catch up or bored out of our minds.

We tend to have an adversarial relationship with time—we think of time as the master and us as its slaves. This paradigm "pits us against time ... At the extreme, time becomes our persecutor, and we think of ourselves as its victim. Since time feels like an ever-present entity hovering in the background of our lives, we come to feel that we're victims of an entity that's always there all the time. Such a view is dangerous to our health, disastrous for our business, and ruinous to our relationships with family and friends."[72]

You and I may not have literal pharaohs whipping us into making bricks like the ancient Jews had to endure in Egypt. But in today's culture we are allowing ourselves to be slaves to the masters of our technologies, our over-commitments, our drive for wealth and material comforts, our status and positions, our possessions, and sometimes even our relationships. And all of these entities revolve around our use of time.

Consequently, our self-identities have become muddied. Our priorities confused. Our senses of value and worth misplaced. Our dreams misguided. We've flipped the hierarchy upside down, with us as the victims with no control and all these other pieces as our masters pushing and prodding us for more.

With all this in mind, Abraham Heschel concludes his paragraph with a profound alternate way of being in time that pays unparalleled dividends. Into the midst of the tempestuous oceans of "time and toil," where we feel tossed around like helpless rag dolls, comes a harbor of stillness—the sabbath—a strategic stop—that has the potential of reinstalling us as sovereigns in the world of time.

Think about this powerful paradigm and practice. Every seven days, for a 24 hour period of time, we choose the gift of time in which to remind ourselves that we are not slaves in bondage to time, we are not victims to time. We are sovereigns with the promise and capacity to shape time to serve us in what matters most to us.

The safe harbor comes automatically every seven days. But we have to choose to sail into it in order to enjoy its multi-layered benefits. That choice is an act of faith and trust—stopping is never easy; there are so many things still left undone at the end of the week—but in this radical act of trust we choose to sail into the harbor because we believe whatever loss we fear we might face as a result will be far less than our experience of being restored, empowered, and renewed for what lies ahead.

Imagine this powerful paradigm shift for the ancient Jews every Sabbath. Six days of enduring pharaoh's slave masters and their whips. Six days of backbreaking brick building, with every moment reinforcing the ugly reality of slavery and bondage to a foreign power. Six days of feeling like their lives and time do not belong to themselves.

Then comes the Sabbath ... when these workers would shut that world away for 24 hours. In community they would celebrate their truth—"Pharaoh might think he controls us and our destiny, but we are not slaves; we are free people with a God-given destiny. We are sovereigns in the world of time because nothing can take away our value, our worth, our identity. We are not victims. We choose our response. We choose our destiny. What we do with our time during Sabbath carries through to how we approach time and our attitude toward time during the other six days. We choose."

Every Sabbath, they were not just washing off the mud that had accumulated on their bodies during the week; they were also washing away the mud from their minds. Cleaning off the lenses of their hearts so they could see clearly again.

In this way, the Sabbath all down through Jewish history has been a practice of resistance and alternative. Walter Bruggemann, a highly respected Christian theologian and prolific author, in his book *The Sabbath as Resistance: Saying No to the Culture of Now*, puts it this way:

> The Sabbath all down through Jewish history has been a practice of resistance and alternative.

"In our contemporary context of the rat race of anxiety, the celebration of Sabbath is an act of both resistance and alternative. It is resistance because it is a visible insistence that our lives are not defined by the production and consumption of commodity goods. Such an act of resistance requires enormous intentionality and communal reinforcement amid the barrage of seductive pressures from the insatiable insistences of the market, with its intrusions into every part of our life from the family to the national budget ... But Sabbath is not only resistance. It is alternative ... The alternative on offer is the awareness and practice of the claim that we are situated on the receiving end of the gifts of 'Life' (God)."[73]

So what does a weekly sabbath practice empower you to resist? What alternative way of being does sabbath inspire you to step into?

First, you are resisting the notion that time is your master and you are its slave. This weekly space in time is set aside to help you remember that you are in control of your life. No one else, no matter what position or authority they might have in your life, can dictate how you feel or what you can choose. You are not a victim of time.

Deliberately carving out these 24 hours from your busy schedule shows a high level of trust in your life and your use of time. You may feel at first like you're missing out on important things on your to-do list by taking a whole day away—especially if you choose to include the putting away of your technology during this sabbath time. Wow, who can survive that kind of radical exclusion?

But this practice becomes an act of faith in the truth that when you devote time to your highest priorities—the priority of shaping your way of being in the world by paying attention to yourself; to your most important relationships; to the wider world in which you live; to activities that restore, renew, and revitalize your whole being and the being of others—you are magnifying your capacity to show up more powerfully in the other six days. Counterintuitively, taking this sabbath time, in truth, expands what's possible in your other time. You become the master of time, treasure, and technology. You are choosing acts of resistance against being defined by those things.

Second, you are reinforcing your true identity—that you are not simply a consumer or producer or user of technology. Your highest purpose in life isn't consumption or production or mastering the tools of your trade. You are meant for way more than those. Your worth, value, and significance are found in your identity as a human being, a global citizen of the human race with the capacity to transform darkness into light, self-centeredness into compassion, hate into love, nationalism into internationalism, and scarcity into abundance.

> Your highest purpose in life isn't consumption or production or mastering the tools of your trade. You are meant for way more than those.

The Jews during the Holocaust had a phrase they used to describe how they faced such horror and deprivation. Referring to the Sabbath, they said, "More than the Jews have kept the Sabbath, the Sabbath has kept the Jews."

This weekly practice, even in the midst of such suffering, was a continual reinforcement of their true identity that was under constant bombardment and test. When they remembered the Sabbath, they remembered who they were.

And third, the alternative way of being that this weekly practice enhances is an attitude of gratitude. When you are faced with the continual temptation during the weekly rat race (the "tempestuous ocean of time and toil") to strive for more in order to be successful and happy, sabbath provides intentional time to practice contentment. "In this moment, I have everything I need."

As neuroscientists remind us, the most impactful physiological and emotional path toward peace is the practice of gratitude. Gratitude taps into and stimulates the highest functioning part of the brain.

I can't tell you how many times, when my wife, Shasta, and I are taking sabbath walks, no matter how discouraging and disillusioning our previous week has been, when we intentionally take 10–20 minutes to express gratitude for everything we can think of and see all around us, the emotional part of us returns to a place of peace, joy, and contentment. Gratitude is always a game-changer for us—even when we start out not wanting to do it. By the end, our emotional and spiritual groundedness have been restored.

> The most impactful physiological and emotional path toward peace is the practice of gratitude. Gratitude taps into and stimulates the highest functioning part of the brain.

Choosing to take weekly sabbath time, concludes Abraham Heschel, reinstalls us as sovereigns in the world of time. This practice reminds us how we can take these kinds of attitudes and behaviors related to time into the rest of the six days of the week. We are not victims. We get to choose how we show up. We get to choose freedom instead of bondage. And no one can take away our inner freedom unless we let them.

What could this island of stillness, this safe harbor, look like for you? How could the regular strategic stop of sabbath restore and reignite the best parts of yourself, your relationships, and your whole environment?

PERSONAL PAUSES

⏸ Identify some specific activities during your sabbath strategic stop that would help remind you of where your value and worth come from, who your true identity is, what your dreams and hopes are, and what matters most to you that tends to get muddied during the busy work week. What would you want to stop doing? And what would you want to do? Some examples could include the following:

Stop doing:
- a technology detox
- a choice to take a pause from being a consumer
- a choice to be work-free (and/or productivity-free)
- What weighs you down during the week that you could let go of during this sabbath strategic stop?

To do:
- engaging in journaling and personal reflection (you can utilize many of the questions raised in this chapter)
- keeping a gratitude journal
- attending a workshop on a topic you are curious about
- meaningful time with friends
- staying in touch with extended family
- special family time
  - outdoor activities such as nature walks, joining a protest gathering or volunteering for a cause you support, savoring a meal in a special restaurant or café, playground time, going to a museum or zoo
  - indoor family activities such as games, singing or playing instruments, doing hobbies together, watching a TV show or movie
  - Consider establishing meaningful rituals to demarcate this time—lighting candles, turning on music, a special meal, expressions of gratitude, a special toast. Plan your activities ahead of time and be prepared—this allows for anticipation and expectation beforehand and utilizing everyone's energy in enjoying the activity when it comes.

TEAM PAUSES

⏸ Though the goal for this kind of sabbath strategic stop might not necessarily mean taking a weekly time off with the whole team, how could the team refocus everyone on the deepest parts of life, like core values, mission and purpose, building healthier connections with each other, personal growth, and development? These strategic stops might take the form of:

- A day or multi-day retreat off-site
- A mini-retreat on-site
- An individual session planned regularly with the above emphases
- Join up with other teams in the company and bring in a motivational speaker on personal and professional growth to inspire and facilitate meaningful interaction

⏸ For these stops to be impactful, what would you want to stop doing and to do? For example:

Stop doing:
- Lay aside the normal project(s) agendas with all the concerns, worries, anxieties, fears, and obsession with productivity
- Establish a technology fast so everyone can be fully present without unnecessary distractions
- Put on hold all feelings of mutual competition—which could mean during this time not engaging in highly competitive activities where there is a winner and a loser

To do:
- Teambuilding activities that foster the three requirements of healthy relationships—positivity, consistency, and vulnerability—to increase self-awareness, relational empathy, and innovative collaboration
- Engage in a volunteer activity with the team

- Adopting another team in the organization to do nice things for—giving notes of encouragement and appreciation, surprising them with a lunch at work, offering to be helpful in their projects, planning an activity together to get to know each other more—with the goal of breaking down the silos that so often exist between teams, departments, and levels of leadership

Solidify the Ballast of Your Leadership and Organization

In the autumn of 1992, Michael Plant, a popular American sailor, set out on a solo crossing of the North Atlantic Ocean from the United States to France. He was an expert who had circumnavigated the globe alone more than once. His midsized sailboat, the *Coyote*, was state-of-the-art constructed and equipped, from hull to mast to sails to navigational and electronic equipment. As far as colleagues and friends and family were concerned, Michael Plant had everything necessary to achieve success on his voyage.

Eleven days into the trip, all contact with him was lost. A massive search was launched. Days went by—no sightings, no radio contact, nothing, even from his top-of-the-line emergency position-indicating radio beacon. And then came the news that no one had ever expected: the *Coyote* was found, floating upside down, 450 miles northwest of the Azores Islands. No sign of Plant, relayed the crew of a freighter that had made the discovery.

The sailing community was surprised that the sailboat was discovered upside down in the water. Sailboats don't normally capsize. They're built to take the most vigorous pounding a sea can offer, and even when knocked over on their side or even upside down, they naturally right themselves. Why this anomaly?

Sailboats are designed for maximum stability in strong winds by having more weight below the waterline. That's one of the purposes of the keel. Alter that ratio and strong wind poses a serious threat. So when the *Coyote* was built, an additional 8,000-pound weight was bolted to the keel in order to provide far more weight below the waterline than even normal. That amount of ballast should have assured stability.

But when the *Coyote* was discovered on that fateful day, the four-ton weight on the keel was missing. Obviously, then, the boat's stability had been seriously compromised. So the first wave or wind of any magnitude became the probable deathblow. And a very capable, experienced, and much-admired yachtsman was lost at sea.

Not enough weight below the waterline. A storm blows. Life lost.

We live in a culture that puts extreme emphasis on what people can see rather than on what can't been seen—our accomplishments, productivity, the next new shiny thing, stock values, making money, spending money. We spend more time on the externals than the internals, but it's what's on the inside—character, soul, heart, mission, purpose, core values: the below-the-waterline issues—that creates significant ballast.

So when the storms of life blow—and they always do at some point—we don't have the necessary ballast to ride it out safely. We become compromised. We fold. We capsize and sometimes don't recover. At best, we simply struggle on, trying to survive and function at minimum capacity, as opposed to really living, flourishing, and being fulfilled and effective at every level.

There's an ancient scripture that asks, "What will it profit a person if they should gain the whole world but lose their own soul?"

In other words, you can design what appears to be the strongest, most successful organization in the world—with stock values shooting sky-high, and stakeholders making insane amounts of money, and products outselling the competition—but if you've lost the soul, the heart of your mission and purpose, the character of your company, and are destroying your people in the process, what is your gain? You end up losing, especially when the fierce winds blow, because you have no depth, no ballast, no character to your organization. And there's nothing to pull you through to avoid the inevitable collapse or deterioration or downward spiral.

Here's the reality: an organization is only as healthy and vibrant as the people in it. Before you and I can lead others, we must first lead ourselves.

"New life emerges not from strategy but from character. Before realizing this, you might think that making plans, devising blueprints for your future or whatever, are the keys to the path ahead. But our real keys to victory are internal. Your state of doing must be matched by the state of your being, or the incongruity will sabotage even your most brilliant plans."[74]

> An organization is only as healthy and vibrant as the people in it. Before you and I can lead others, we must first lead ourselves.

Leaders must not fixate on hard skills to the neglect of soft skills. It's these so-called soft skills—paying attention to the human-being side of the organization—that build the appropriate ballast in the organization.

So how does one go about paying attention to what matters most? How can we bring congruence and alignment to all parts of our lives and organizations so we move forward fully alive and on point with a clear sense of transformational purpose? How do we make sure that our organization doesn't lose its necessary ballast?

Five Ways to Deepen Your Ballast

Though Dr. Howard Thurman isn't talking specifically about organizations, his wisdom can certainly be applied to leaders and their organizations. Notice the five ways he describes to build depth and transformation. Central to each of these strategies is the significance of engaging in strategic stops.

"All travelers, somewhere along the way, find it necessary to check their course, to see how they are doing. We wait until we are sick, or shocked into stillness, before we do the commonplace thing of getting our bearings. And yet, we wonder why we are depressed, why we are unhappy, why we lose our friends, why we are ill-tempered. This condition we pass on to our children, our spouses and significant others, our associates, our friends. Cultivate the mood to linger. ... Who knows? Life may whisper to you in the quietness what Life has been trying to say to you, oh, for so long a time."[75]

1. Know Your Purpose and Communicate It Often

One of the primary characteristics that keeps employees engaged in their jobs is for them to know how what they do every day contributes to the ultimate purpose of the company. People have to experience purposeful meaning in their work in order to be engaged, fulfilled, and enjoy their jobs. In fact, more and more millennials are choosing jobs based to a high degree on whether or not they believe in or feel inspired by the mission and vision of the company.

The challenge in today's workplace culture, according to Gallup's most recent State of the American Workplace study, is that employees are increasingly losing confidence in their leaders, substantially over this very issue of vision. Notice this sobering description:

> "There is an urgency for leaders to define and convey their vision more clearly—and rally employees around it. Gallup data reveal an unsettling pattern in the U.S. workplace. Employees have little belief in their company's leadership. We have found that just:
> - 22% of employees strongly agree the leadership of their organization has a clear direction for the organization.
> - 15% of employees strongly agree the leadership of their organization makes them enthusiastic about the future.
> - 13% of employees strongly agree the leadership of their organization communicates effectively with the rest of the organization."[76]

People are making decisions about staying in their companies based upon whether or not they are compelled and inspired by the leaders and their overall vision of the company's purpose. The ancient proverb about people perishing without vision is so accurate in our contemporary culture—employees are disengaging in high percentages because of lack of vision and the lack of joy in what they're being asked to do.

The point is, there is a direct correlation between vision, communication of vision, and employee satisfaction and respect for leadership.

Truth is, in the end, it is the shared responsibility of leaders, managers, and all employees to understand, stay focused on, and be empowered to move forward by their vision of the organization's North Star. This is why planning regular strategic stops for this opportunity of reminder and celebration of purpose is so vital to organizational success.

> There is a direct correlation between vision, communication of vision, and employee satisfaction and respect for leadership.

Imagine sailors navigating their boat without a clear picture of where they're going. Imagine them overcoming obstacles without being able to see landmarks along the way to check their course. Imagine them never knowing where the points of the compass are and where they are in relationship to that and to their ultimate destination. The outcome of these predicaments would be sailors simply sailing around in the open waters using the wind and currents to go anywhere. If you don't know where you're going, anywhere works fine. But races and explorations are never won by going just anywhere.

> It's one thing to know your destination (purpose). It's another thing to have effective strategies that will get you there.

2. Check Your Course Regularly

Dr. Thurman called this "getting your bearings." Is where we're currently headed going to get us to our destination? Are we still on track?

A business author calls this "operationalizing your purpose." It's one thing to know your destination (purpose). It's another thing to have effective strategies that will get you there. This is about clearly seeing where you are at any given moment in relation to your destination and then determining whether the strategies you've developed are achieving your purpose.

One of the significant factors in operationalizing your purpose is to develop a fluid and dynamic ability to shift directions when necessary.

This is where sailing is a helpful metaphor. Sailors are clear on this—we can't create the wind, we can't change its direction; we can only leverage it. Our task is to use the wind from whatever direction it's coming to chart a course that ultimately gets us as efficiently and effectively as possible to our destination. This tactic is known as tacking.

Because a sailboat can never steer directly into the wind—it only has the capacity to move at a 45-degree angle from either side of the windward point of sail—we have to tack back and forth across the wind in order to get to where we want go. We zigzag upwind.

Which means we can never be married to any one zig or zag or point of sail. Even though we may really be enjoying the tack we're on—leveraging the wind in ways that are exhilarating and energizing, the boat heeling over in the wind, the wind blowing in our faces, adrenaline pumping through our systems—we simply can't remain forever on that tack. We have to shift directions. We have to be able to be flexible and dynamic.

In an organizational setting, I refer to this as developing corporate and personal plasticity. We must nurture the capacity to shift strategies in changing conditions. Our purpose doesn't change—our purpose is based upon our unique relevance in the world. Keeping this vision alive helps us stay focused on where we're going and why. But if we don't shift tactics, if we don't develop an operational nimbleness, we can become victims to the changing winds all around us.

A good example of this is the pepper trade industry in the 19th century. The original purpose of pepper was to preserve food. And then that purpose was disrupted—not by a better spice, but by refrigeration. Pepper's purpose was co-opted by a new and more effective strategy. And the pepper industry ended up not being able to shift with this major change.

Think about all the disruptions to established industries in the last few decades. Look what ride-sharing businesses have done to the taxi-cab industry. What about how the internet has disrupted broadcast TV, cable TV, and print journalism, as well as traditional publishing? And the impact smartphones have had on mobile computing.

The winds blow sometimes with gale force. But only those who have a deep ballast anchored in a firm sense of purpose and mission along with this strategic plasticity—the ability to be nimble and the willingness to shift tactics—can survive.

Good sailing is about managing and using your resources strategically to get where you're going.

> Only those who have a deep ballast anchored in a firm sense of purpose and mission along with this strategic plasticity—the ability to be nimble and the willingness to shift tactics—can survive.

"Corporate plasticity is the ability to collaborate in the pursuit of a common objective and rapidly reconfigure to face new challenges—which is of course essential to operationalizing purpose in the real world, where conditions constantly change and people's actions may yield unintended as well as intended consequences.

"Plasticity needs to be actively nurtured by leaders who free people to be guided not solely by management dictates but also by the company's clarity of purpose. Jorgen Vig Knudstorp, the CEO who revitalized the Lego brand, often told his employees, 'Thank you for doing all the things I never told you to do.'"[77]

3. Cultivate the Mood to Linger

This is the intentional choice to embed in the leadership, personal, and organizational culture pauses that are strategic opportunities to refocus, to remember (or, as that word literally means, re-member—bringing all the pieces of ourselves, the whole of our organizations, back together again the way they have been designed to be).

Notice the three aspects to this strategic stop process that Dr. Thurman describes: cultivate the mood to linger. This refers to a specific kind of intentionality. In other words, the most effective and transformational culture in organizations doesn't just happen or appear out of thin air. Healthy, people-driven, powerful-outcome-resulting culture is created and shaped by leadership.

"Cultivate" implies priority, active encouragement, facilitation, setting aside specific time, and then the choice to keep doing it again and again.

"Mood" implies the work of developing a specific kind of atmosphere and environment conducive to personal, leadership, and team development and growth. It involves all the senses; it's very holistic in its methodology and experience.

> The most effective and transformational culture in organizations doesn't just happen or appear out of thin air. Healthy, people-driven, powerful-outcome-resulting culture is created and shaped by leadership.

And "linger" suggests that the atmosphere is so positive and life-giving that people want to spend time there—there isn't the typical rush to move on to the next thing. Lingering is a hugely significant human way of being that implies a savoring enhanced by available time and attention.

Each of these three descriptors builds on the one before it. And together they represent a total package of creating a place where people feel fully alive and where they love to work.

Cultivation is a farming concept. This agricultural metaphor reveals some significant actions necessary for increasing the fertility of the organizational soil (culture).

There's an ancient story about a farmer who goes out to plant some seed. "As he scattered it across his field, some seeds fell on a footpath, and the birds came and ate them. Other seeds fell on shallow soil with underlying rock. The plants sprang up quickly, but they soon wilted beneath the hot sun and died because the roots had no nourishment in the shallow soil. Other seeds fell among weeds and thorns that shot up and choked out the tender blades. But some seeds fell on fertile soil and produced a crop that was thirty, sixty, and even a hundred times as much as had been planted, a harvest beyond the farmer's wildest dreams."[78]

Notice the four kinds of soil in this story: smooth, shallow, thorny, and fertile. Here's where this ancient story is useful as an evaluation tool for organizational culture and growth.

The smooth soil is essentially a footpath that has become hardened because of people walking on it again and again. It represents a lot of activity—busyness. Sounds like much of our society. We are living in a nonstop world that has invaded our organizations from the top leaders to every employee and worker.

It's like the cartoon I saw once where a man was at his doctor's office for a check-up. The doctor's prognosis is, "I diagnose your problem as a biterminal combustion of the paraffinic illuminator. In other words, Charlie, you're burning your candle at both ends."

Does that sound familiar to you? Our individual lives have become nothing more than footpaths. Our team sessions and our leadership styles revolve around everyone's busyness. We are driven by productivity agendas to the extent that we can never slow down. We have to be pushing and moving at all times and at all costs.

This smooth soil, however, does not produce a fertile environment. The seed may get planted, but then it gets trampled down. The seed never gets an opportunity to sink below the surface and germinate. And so the birds of distraction come and eat it.

Futurist David Zach calls this state of being hyper-living—skimming along the surface of life. There's no real purpose, no depth, no fertility. And there's no ballast to survive the heavy winds.

The shallow soil is essentially soil that has only a few inches of topsoil with bedrock beneath. So seeds might sprout up like normal, but because there's no depth, the seeds sending their roots to find moisture come up without proper nourishment. The roots hit rock. And though the seeds germinate and grow seedlings, when the sun burns bright, the baby plants die from lack of depth and nourishment.

I've seen many an organization that relies on emotionalism and superficiality. It's the classic feel-good place to work—lots of fun, games, positive activities. There's a tendency to always be attracted to the next shiny thing—the latest trendy program or methodology. There's no room for anything that doesn't feel good. These leaders are often addicted to adrenaline—the excitement of the hunt, the battle, the win, the successful launching of a new product.

I spent some time coaching a leader like this. He was so good at leading through chaos that he actually (and probably somewhat unconsciously) ended up creating chaos so he could come in and be the savior of the organization. He had allowed this way of being to embed itself in his identity. "I am the great deliverer from chaos and confusion."

What he didn't see—until I pointed it out—was that he was also wounding and hurting a lot of people who were working for him. They were managing as effectively as possible to bring things to a place of greater peace, harmony, and effectiveness—until he started new distractions and subsequent crises, upending the harmony and peace. You can imagine what this culture and environment was doing to the people who worked there. They were under a high level of continual stress—never knowing when the next crisis would emerge—so they could never feel at peace and under control. They could never feel like they were doing a good enough job. He always had to come in and save the day—from a crisis he himself had created.

Working in a culture that is either fun and games (avoiding disappointment, discouragement, or struggle) or crisis management is living with shallow soil. The seed of purpose can never grow and fully develop because it never goes deep enough to find nourishment. This is an organization that will ultimately fold and capsize when the heavy winds blow. There's not the necessary ballast and depth.

The thorny soil is fertile enough for seeds to germinate and grow. The challenge is, however, that weeds grow prolifically as well. And if not taken care of or removed, the weeds end up choking out the life of the plants.

In this ancient story about the farmer and the soils, the weeds are said to represent the worries of this life and the lures of wealth. Interesting. In other words, weeds are attitudes, beliefs, and obsessions that have the potential of squeezing and choking out life itself. How? They keep the seedling, the young plant, from getting necessary nutrition and nourishment. The stock and stem are squeezed and choked so that the moisture cannot rise all the way to the upper and outer leaves and blossoms. Blockages. Reduced life. Ultimate collapse.

So what would this look like in an organization? What are blocks that can be erected that would keep every level of the organization from receiving life-giving nourishment?

Could it be a lack of vision about its purpose that ultimately leads to the draining of energy from every employee? A lack of communication of the purpose? It has a purpose, but people simply aren't hearing about it regularly or might be hearing about it in a way that isn't compelling or inspiring.

Could it be an environment that is centered solely on its products and services to the exclusion of its people and team development and growth? A lack of opportunities for workers to develop their own potential?

Could it be a culture in which there is a complete separation between people's work lives and their personal lives? "What happens at home stays at home—don't bring it to work. Here at work, we pay you to think only about work. So no matter what your life worries and fears are, we don't want you having to think about them here at work. Don't get distracted!" In other words, the world is totally binary as opposed to holistic.

Or could it be the opposite of that—a complete blending of personal and professional in a way that work is always invading personal time at home? The expectation that you are always on, even when you're not at work. You can never leave your work behind.

Could it be that the company is obsessed solely with the financial bottom line? That the stakeholders are the most important demographic? That your identity and worth are based solely upon the size of your paycheck and stock options or the product success of your company?

Could it be that leadership is paying attention to the loudest voices, external and internal, to the neglect of the average worker, who often feels like their voice carries no weight or significance?

Could it be that the organization tends to run at such hyperspeed that there are never strategic stops carved into life when people can pause, breathe, become more grounded in their humanity, and focus on what's most important—where people can develop deeper self-awareness, relational empathy, and purpose-driven outcomes?

An organization that doesn't regularly weed its growth environment is going to remain superficial and ultimately allow those weeds to choke out its life. No depth. No ballast. No substantial strength to withstand the winds.

In contrast, the fertile soil is a place of vast difference. Regular weeding is done. Stones removed. Dirt cultivated, fertilized, and watered adequately. And the seeds grow and develop to their maximum capacity, yielding a hugely productive harvest.

Imagine working in an organization where every person can achieve their fullest potential; where everyone counts and matters; where everyone is asked to contribute their best strengths; where limiting beliefs are patiently identified and overcome; where there exists a deep respect for and honor of each other; where people are encouraged, supported, and maximized to be their best; where there is a palpable patience with the process and journey of people's lives; where innovation and creativity are valued from everyone; and where people are proud to be a part of its purpose and mission, willing to work hard to support it and make it happen.

> An organization that doesn't regularly weed its growth environment is going to remain superficial and ultimately allow those weeds to choke out its life. No depth. No ballast. No substantial strength to withstand the winds

What would it feel like to work in that place? What would it take for you to cultivate the mood to linger where you work? What would need to happen for that to be a possibility? What changes would you need to make? What changes would your leaders need to make?

4. Fix Your Blind Spots

Remember the world-class sailor Michael Plant from the beginning of this chapter? His sailboat was discovered floating upside down in the middle of the Atlantic Ocean. He was never found.

The sailing community was both shocked and baffled. How could someone like Plant be lost at sea? He had successfully circumnavigated the globe several times by himself. Why had this time been different, especially with a boat boasting state-of-the-art equipment and engineering?

Upon further investigation, it was discovered that Michael had never registered his EPIRB—emergency position-indicating radio beacon—with the Coast Guard. Which meant that when he got into trouble—most likely because of a major storm—he was never able to utilize that important piece of equipment to send signals to the Coast Guard about his current position. So he excluded himself from the possibility of being discovered and rescued in time.

Why would he fail to register this life-saving piece of technology?

Some of his friends and other sailing experts believe that his arrogance is what ultimately caught up to him. He was completely confident—most probably overconfident—in his abilities. After all, he had done this route before. Surely he could handle whatever came at him. Why should he worry about a small detail like registering a piece of equipment?

Arrogance and overconfidence, combined with the loss of the needed extra ballast on his keel, facing the worst winds and waves of his life—all together served to overwhelm him and his boat. And a skilled sailor was forever lost.

You should never underestimate the power of blind spots. We all have them, whether or not we have identified them.

I've seen that leaders, no matter how successful they are, are especially prone to blind spots. They have achieved a level of success and often become surrounded by people who end up, sometimes without realizing it, telling the leader what they believe the leader wants to hear. After all, no one wants to risk losing his or her job.

> Leaders, no matter how successful they are, especially prone to blind spots.

And because of the success, the leader automatically assumes that he or she can continue using the same strategies and professional narratives to keep their success growing indefinitely. So they often never search for or get told the wider truth about themselves and how they're coming across.

Unless the limiting belief and blind spot are addressed, the leader has a built-in limitation. And that limitation—that lack of ballast—will often cause ineffectiveness or derail and sometimes even destroy the leader, especially when the difficult winds blow. Integrity—which means living in alignment with the truth about who you are and spending more time paying attention to character issues below the waterline of your life—is the only antidote to collapse when times get rough and tough.

Here are some limiting beliefs and blind spots I've noticed in leaders. Can you relate to any of them?

- **I am invincible and can do no wrong.**
  This is essentially the god-complex that often appears in people with great power and influence. The flip side of this belief is, "I have no power and agency on my own. Nothing I do is enough." So

the leader works extra hard to overcompensate for that feeling of a lack of personal power. Control. Aggression. Arrogance. Lack of responsibility or admission of wrong. Whatever it takes to bolster the feeling of invincibility and power.

- **I know what's best for the people in my life.**
  This often comes from a need to control people and situations. Beneath it is a deep insecurity about self and capacity manifested in an overconfidence in their own knowledge and abilities. The flip side is, "I have no voice—what I think and say don't matter enough. I will be silent." The result is often allowing others to run over them or control them.

- **People are to be used as tools for my success.**
  Few people actually speak this out loud. But in this belief, relationships are secondary in importance to personal success and power. Only the strong and powerful succeed. This often stems from a fear of being controlled and losing personal freedom.

- **My image is the most important part of me. I need to manage it because image is everything.**
  This belief results in a leader spending an exorbitant amount of energy and attention on the externals—what people can see and notice, what people think about him or her. What gets left behind in priority are the internals, the character issues, the motivations driving behaviors, as well as the behaviors that no one else sees.

- **I can't trust anyone because they'll betray me.**
  Having been hurt or betrayed in the past, this belief tries to build a wall around self for protection. It often manifests in aggressive and arrogant behaviors that keep people at a controllable distance.

- **Failure is not an option—I have to work harder than everyone else to not fail.**
  Beneath this limiting belief is the fear of inadequacy—the fear of letting others down and confirming this belief about themselves. So it has constructed an identity that refuses failure at all cost and centers on success as the basis for self-esteem and self-worth.

- **I'm not good enough the way I am.**

  This is a tandem belief to the previous one. It is the foundation for the fear of failure, the need to control, and the obsession with success. It stems from early messages of not being able to please the most important people in our lives. It manifests in either withdrawal tendencies (lack of assertiveness) or aggressive and overconfident behaviors.

- **I can't pursue my dreams because I have to provide for my family, which needs stability, not uncertainty.**

  This too is from the fear of failure, of not being a good provider, of not being able to carve out a new life based upon dreams and passions—"What if I fail and don't succeed in this new venture?" It shows a lack of confidence in self and capacity from the fear of risks. It can often come from an overdeveloped sense of responsibility to others rather than to one's self—the inability to find that balance between the two. Leaders who embrace this limiting belief often experience a build-up of internal resentment toward life, family, and peers for blocking the fulfillment of their dreams. It's often easier to blame others than to take responsibility for their own fear-based choices. Because in the final analysis, none of us is a victim to our circumstances or people in our lives. We have agency. We just need to take it.

Do you resonate with any of these limiting beliefs? Can you identify how any of them show up in your life? If you were to give this list to the people closest to you, would they identify any of these in you? How would they describe blind spots you are manifesting?

> Every limiting belief manifests itself in blind-spot behaviors...Left unchecked, these beliefs and behaviors can wreak havoc on the leader's life and the lives of the people that surround him or her

Every limiting belief manifests itself in blind-spot behaviors. And because the belief isn't always noticed by the leader, the blind spots aren't easily visible either. Left unchecked, these beliefs and behaviors can wreak havoc on the leader's life and the lives of the people that surround him or her.

5. Build Ongoing Relationships with Supportive, Wise, and Honest People

For this reason, I believe it's vital for leaders to belong to a small group of trusted and wise people for the purpose of mutually sharing transparently and with accountability their journeys of life and work. Some groups are called Masterminds, others are support groups or peer groups. Sometimes this support system takes the form of an accountability partner—someone you trust to be a mutual witness to your whole life, with whom you share transparently and authentically, and who comes to know you so well that they can hold the space in each conversation with encouragement, honesty, and wisdom.

Until leaders put themselves in environments where they can be truly honest and authentic, showing their whole selves and being loved and supported in the process, it's far too easy for them to live with facades and end up believing that those masks represent their true selves. Our image-consultant masks rule the day, every day, until we learn how to silence those voices in favor of authenticity and personal liberation. We need others to help us on this path.

I remember finishing my sharing time during one of my monthly Mastermind sessions and having my peers respond, "Greg, thank you for your share. We've never seen you this energized, passionate, confident, and powerful before. You wear it well. You finally dropped your mask and became real."

I thought to myself, "Thanks for the compliment?" From my vantage point, I had been as real as ever for quite a while, losing my image consultant with this group of trusted peers. And yet, here they were reflecting that they had still been seeing my mask until now.

Their validation of what they saw and felt from me in my sharing that day was incredibly meaningful to me. And their honesty helped me process with them how they had seen my image consultant at work even in this trusted group. I was able to see myself through their eyes, realizing that my insecurities and fears were still showing up. This became a huge turning point for me. Moving forward, I kept my focus on that amazing feeling of honesty, confidence and power I had during my share as I continued navigating my way through my process of liberation. I wouldn't have seen this reality as clearly without their supportive feedback.

I have been extremely intentional about pulling people like this into my life orbit—it is a nonnegotiable for me—people like my wife, first and foremost; my two best friends; my Mastermind group; and coaches I've hired to help me process where I'm going and how I can get there in ways that leverage who I am and how I'm wired. I connect with them all regularly, by phone or in person. Time and again, their loving care for me has empowered me to step more fully into my authentic self. Time and again, they've held up a mirror for me to see who I am and how I'm doing, and to notice areas of growth that I'm missing. And then they've compassionately and encouragingly supported me in taking necessary steps for improvement. I always know they're cheering me on like I am with them. We have each other's best interests at heart. We are each other's biggest fans. What's not to love?

> Leaders need this kind of mutual support to empower them to be their best selves, to do the necessary weeding and cultivating in order to develop more depth and ballast.

Who do you have in your life that you regularly share yourself with? Do you feel completely safe in that relationship so that you are honest and transparent? Are you open to supportive feedback? Do you have people in your life whom you trust to challenge you and your beliefs and your ways of being as well as encourage and validate your progress and growth?

Leaders need this kind of mutual support to empower them to be their best selves, to do the necessary weeding and cultivating in order to develop more depth and ballast. Why? So their leadership can be on point and on purpose, even when the strong winds blow. And then they can lead their organizations authentically and successfully when times are tough, empowering their organizations to build depth and ballast too.

Here's the way Marianne Williamson puts it:

"If you fail at the art of being human and staying human, you recklessly court disaster … What I've learned, to the extent to which I've been successful at any of this, is that the path of right living is walked one moment at a time. Whether you show up for life as a jerk or a saint has little to do with belief or theology; it has to do with personal integrity. We aren't transformed in our hearts by mere belief, because belief isn't of the heart. The heart's transformation is not attained through the mind—it's attained through surrender, authenticity, forgiveness, faith, honesty, acceptance, vulnerability, humility, willingness, nonjudgment, and other characterological values that have to be learned and relearned continuously."[79]

A leader's journey of authenticity, character, and confidence is not for the faint of heart. It takes great courage. Persistence. Openness. Our organizations need good and authentic leaders. Being on purpose, with a compelling vision, with core values that empower rather than diminish its people, is the strongest foundation possible. Fertile soil. Abundant harvest. And none of this can be accomplished alone.

I used to own a 16-foot Snipe sailboat. It was incredibly nimble, fast, and definitely tricky to handle because of its instability. Unlike a bigger sailboat, the Snipe doesn't have a keel with heavy ballast. It has a dagger board that is lowered and raised in the middle of the cockpit. It doesn't provide ballast as much as a counterbalance to the force of the wind on the sails. In other words, it keeps the boat from simply sliding sideways in order to keep it moving forward. The weight balance is achieved by the people in the boat. You've seen pictures of sailors all on one side of the boat, leaning way over the edge in order to add as much weight as possible to the upside to keep the boat stable in strong winds. It's a beautiful sight. And it's an exhilarating experience.

My youngest son, Julian, and I were sailing in heavy winds on Lake Washington near downtown Seattle. It was a perfect sailing day. I was skippering, and Julian was manning the headsail and providing ballast by always moving to the opposite side of the boat from me or from the wind. Our tacks back and forth were getting smoother and quicker with each one. Our teamwork was superb. We were having a blast!

And then we approached another tack into the wind. As per usual, I gave the command "Ready to come about!" which meant that we were preparing to tack by getting into position. And then I yelled, "Coming about!"

I steered into and then past the wind. The boat moved quickly. And Julian began his move to the other side to balance my weight. Unfortunately, we both responded a bit too slowly. Our weight remained on the downside of the boat so that by the time the wind hit the opposite sail with force in our new tack, there was no counterbalance.

What happened next was like being in a slow-motion movie scene. The sail got pushed downward toward the water. The boat heeled over farther. And we both fell off the boat straight into the sail, which then pushed the sail farther under the water until the mast turtled—essentially pointing straight down to the lake bottom.

The water was freezing! We swam to the upside-down hull of the boat and held on to the dagger board. And then we heard the voice—it was coming from above—"Do you need help?"

I looked up and saw the Coast Guard. I have no idea how they showed up so quickly. I didn't even know that they had been in the vicinity. But here they were, ready to help.

Now I have just enough pride to want to fix things myself. So I called out, "Thanks for offering. I think we can get this. But if you can stay there in case we need you, that would be great!"

After several tries to right our boat, we finally made it. Bodies still intact. Pride a bit wounded. Cold, shivering, but thankful to be upright again.

Get the ballast wrong and you pay the price. Too little depth and weight below the waterline, or get the wrong balance, and you lose.

> Get the ballast wrong and you pay the price. Too little depth and weight below the waterline, or get the wrong balance, and you lose.

Richard Foster, one of our culture's great spiritual writers and guides, has said, "The desperate need today is not for a great number of intelligent people, or gifted people, but for deep people."

Ballast matters!

The same can be said about leaders and organizations. Learning how to live by paying attention to what's below the surface—the heart and character issues, core values, staying true to your purpose, your North Star, paying attention to the truth of what grounds us and centers us—is what ends up providing stability, ballast, and depth. Ballast matters!

The result is that when the storms of life blow, there's enough internal weight to weather it and end up not just functioning but flourishing. World-renowned sailor Michael Plant hit the biggest storm of his life and lost the battle because he didn't have enough weight below the waterline. Our organizations, our leaders, our employees, none of us can afford to ignore this ratio. The price is simply too high if we do. Ballast matters!

LEADERSHIP PAUSES

⏸ As a leader, how often do you communicate the vision of your organization to your employees? In what specific ways (in person, via video or other visual media, newsletter, email, all-hands gatherings for employees)? How might you add opportunities?

⏸ How do your employees evaluate your communication of the vision and purpose? Are you conveying it in a compelling and inspiring way? What specific ways could you communicate it more often and more effectively?

⏸ Which of the four soils (described in the ancient farming story) best characterizes the environment and culture of your organization—hyper-busy; shallow with no depth (lack of character and values); product-focused rather than people-centric; or well-rounded, grounded, and empowering for everyone?

⏸ Identify four steps you will take to shift your organization's culture to have more depth (ballast)—re-examining your core values and evaluating how aligned you are on every level of your organization, evaluating your employee engagement and establishing ways to increase it, training your internal leaders to be effective coaches to their teams, or providing more professional and personal development opportunities for individuals and teams.

⏸ What personal and professional blind spots might you have that are keeping you from being your best self and leader? Whom do you trust around you to ask the question, "How can I be more effective as a leader in this place? Is there something I'm missing that I need to address to be more effective?"

⏸ Are you a part of a supportive group of peers that meets regularly for mutual growth and accountability? If not, why not? Identify three steps you will commit to taking in order to be a part of such a group.

TEAM PAUSES

⏸ Evaluate your typical team session agendas. What percentage of time is spent on the details of your projects versus people and team dynamics, connectedness, and personal development (hard skills vs. soft skills)? What would it take to balance that ratio?

⏸ Do you know the mission/purpose statement of your organization? Can you state it right now by memory? Can you describe clearly how your everyday work contributes to the organization's mission? How could your clarity be increased? On a scale of 1–5 (1 being non-inspiring, 5 being very motivating), how you would you personally rate the mission and purpose?

⏸ Team sharing questions: "Using the sailing metaphor of tacking back and forth in order to reach your destination, describe a time in your life when you had to tack in order to get to where you wanted to go. Perhaps you encountered an obstacle standing in your way that you had to go around. Though a potentially difficult experience, you ended up looking back and seeing the value of that tack." "Describe a time when your team or company has tacked in order to move forward—you realize the team or company was engaging in corporate plasticity."

⏸ Team sharing question: "Describe two specific ways your team and organizational culture could be cultivated to produce a more fertile soil (environment) that reclaims the human being side of people." What practical steps could your team take to help implement some of these ideas?

⏸ Team sharing questions: "Describe two of your core values— the values that mean the most to you—and some examples of how you live those out in your personal and professional life." "List two of your organization's core values—values that are stated as primary to its life and mission—and some examples of how you see it living those out from day to day."

CONCLUSION

Five Questions to Help You Evaluate Your Strategic Stops

1. Are your strategic stops helping you become more fully alive?

One of my guiding life statements is, "The glory of Life is a human fully alive."[80]

This is the determining issue in all the choices we make. If I make choice X, will it contribute to heightening, deepening, and expanding my life or the lives of others? Or will this diminish life? Will I be able to say afterward that I am more fully alive than before? Fully alive!

Recovering our essential and authentic humanity means making choices that enhance life rather than diminish it. Fully alive.

It's amazing how many people are simply, as one author put it, trying to make it to death safely. That's their top priority in life. Status quo. The walking dead. Like standing on a moving sidewalk in the airport to simply be carried along like everyone else—a mass transportation system that minimizes individual and group effort. Floating along with the current. The antithesis of being fully alive.

The chapters in this book have described the various ways that help people be more fully alive in the workplace, at home, within organizations, in the rough and tumble of life. It has offered nine power pauses—strategic stops—that radically contribute to our sense of well-being, of being fully alive, of being authentically human, and the practices and tools that will enhance life rather than diminish it.

What makes these stops strategic is their focus on developing our capacity to engage in regular physical and emotional rest, leveraging our human systems' recovery systems, self-reflection and self-evaluation, building healthy and empathetic relationships within our teams, identifying and staying focused on personal and organizational purpose, building more depth and ballast in our organizations, and structuring a sabbath experience into our weekly rhythms.

Admittedly, these practices take time and effort. We can't expect their positive outcomes to show up automatically once we express the wish for them. We are being called to engage with life rather than let life pass us by. But that radical act of engagement shows a basic trust in life—that when we devote ourselves to the deepest part of life, we reap rich dividends, as do the people associated with us. Fully alive.

So ask yourself the evaluation question, "Will this strategic stop help me (and any others involved in it) become more fully alive—where we all leave this stop feeling that our lives have been positively developed and not diminished in any way?"

2. Are your strategic stops enhancing your essential human skills?

"Leadership today is about unlearning management and relearning being human."[81] That's a wise perspective from one of today's great leaders, Javier Pladevall, CEO of Volkswagen Audi Retail in Spain.

In the midst of all of our hustle and bustle, we are in danger of losing our essential humanity. The pressure to conform to all the external and sometimes internal messages about what we need to be happy and successful is strong. "Buy this, act like this, own this, offer this, position yourself like this, follow this, believe this, don't believe that, use this formula, go to this, experience this."

> "Leadership today is about unlearning management and relearning being human."

People are losing themselves in the process of living. Conforming is taking precedence over authenticity.

So engaging in regular strategic stops is becoming more and more crucial to recovering our true humanity. We should be asking ourselves—whether we're leaders, individual contributors, parents, single, married, or no matter what stage of life we're in—the fundamental evaluation question, "Is this going to help me be more authentically human?"

In 2013, the giant tech company Google conducted a massive survey of their hiring process to determine what skills end up being the most important in hiring, firing, and promoting practices inside the company. Their hypothesis was that only technologists can understand technology. So those with the highly touted STEM training (Science, Technology, Engineering, Mathematics) would obviously have priority and fit into their company the best.

As it turned out, they discovered that of the eight most important qualities of Google's top employees, STEM expertise came in dead last. Instead, those attributes commonly called soft skills ranked at the top: "being a good coach; communicating and listening well; possessing insights into others (including others' different values and points of view); having empathy toward and being supportive of one's colleagues; being a good critical thinker and problem solver; and being able to make connections across complex ideas."[82]

This kind of research is taking place all over the world with similar results. Success in life is determined by how authentically human people really are. Our ability to relearn the art of being truly human needs to be placed back at the top of our list of priorities.

"STEM skills are vital to the world we live in today, but technology alone, as Steve Jobs famously insisted, is not enough. We desperately need the expertise of those who are educated to the human, cultural, and social as well as the computational."[83]

So an evaluation question for the strategic stops you initiate is, "Are your practices leading you to develop more human capacities, like empathy, respect, curiosity, self-awareness, healthy connections with others, effective communication, active listening, and kindness?" If these are some of the outcomes of your strategic stop practices, then you're on track. If not, you need to carefully re-evaluate the focus of your strategic stops.

3. Are the boundaries of your strategic stops clearly defined?

The latest Pew Research Center report posted results from surveys with teens (ages 13–17) about social media and technology. "As smartphone access has become more prevalent, a growing share of teens now report using the internet on a near-constant basis. Some 45% of teens say they use the internet 'almost constantly,' a figure that has nearly doubled from the 24% who said this in the 2014–2015 survey. [This is a 100% increase in the last three years.] Another 44% say they go online several times a day, meaning roughly nine-in-ten teens go online at least multiple times per day."[84]

What this nonstop usage is leading to, says one author, is that, though these devices seem innocent enough when we interact with them, we are entering "a profoundly fluid temporal universe with no beginning or end and none of the usual boundaries between day and night, work and rest, shopping and non-shopping. The proliferation of mobile communications devices, combined with the global 24/7 economy, is moving us further and further away from the temporal regimes that have kept us sane for centuries and into a zone of perpetual momentum that keeps speeding us up without ever prompting us to stop."[85]

Her phrase "a profoundly fluid temporal universe" is powerfully descriptive. In that universe, we lose all track of time—as in, there are no boundaries that help facilitate a sense of beginning and ending. Our 24/7 accessing of information via smartphones and other media blurs our sense of time and in the end contributes to a belief that all time is the same in quality and priority.

For example, when I see a couple in a restaurant and both people are on their smartphones, no conversation taking place, I realize that they have succumbed to that fluid temporal universe where all time is the same time. No delineation of time. No sense of specialness with that time segment in which they have the opportunity to enjoy each other's company in the restaurant. Perpetual momentum. Sameness. How romantic. Or not.

> Our 24/7 accessing of information via smartphones and other media blurs our sense of time and in the end contributes to a belief that all time is the same in quality and priority.

This is why strategic stops are so vital. We make sure there is a clearly defined beginning and ending. We establish specific rituals to denote the beginning and the end. And what we do during that time is qualitatively different from all other time. We are paying attention to the most important parts of our lives—our human beingness and how we as human beings interact with each other. So that what we do during those specified times ends up bleeding into the other parts of our lives in a most positive, fulfilling, and enhancing way.

I remember with great fondness one of the father-daughter date nights with my daughter Natalie when she was five or six years old. We each got dressed up in nice outfits. I opened the car door for her. We drove up to the big city of Seattle in the evening. It felt very special.

We sat down in a restaurant and ordered big mugs of hot chocolate. The night lights of downtown were twinkling outside the window. I don't remember exactly the content of our conversation. But I remember my feelings in those moments. I felt like the luckiest father in the world, so happy being with her. And there was nothing that could have pulled me away or distracted me. We marked the beginning and the end of that time together. And everything in between was devoted exclusively to each other. It was truly magical.

Since then, Natalie and I have from time to time reminisced about that date night. And whenever I visit Seattle I go to that cafe, take a picture of it, and text it to her.

Meaningful time often needs to be demarcated to preserve the specialness—intentional boundaries that establish the significance and value of that time. When you can, make your strategic stops count.

4. With every strategic stop you initiate, what are you in turn subtracting from your schedule?

We live in an age of excess and choice—and an overabundance of both. Just walk into Costco, a bookstore (remember those buildings that house books for sale?), Safeway, or a mall and look around. Or take a quick tour through Amazon.com.

I have some friends who came back to the United States after several decades of working for an NGO in Africa. I asked them what the biggest adjustment was since returning. They immediately said, "Walking into a grocery store and going up and down the aisles, seeing so many choices and options of the same item. We were completely overwhelmed. And turned off. It seemed so excessive and wasteful after what we had been living with overseas."

This excess and overabundance is contributing to overwhelm and distress. Truth is, we can't just hoard and stockpile, no matter how good the objects of our desires and wants are. We only have a finite space for things physically and emotionally. Our bandwidth is limited.

For example, all the meetings you are asked to attend at work might be good and important. But you don't have time for everything. Every gift you receive at Christmas might be exactly what you were hoping for. But you don't have room in your house or apartment to keep everything you've ever received. Every request people make of you might be just what you've been wanting to do, but you don't have unlimited energy and time to do them all. Right?

Enter the law of subtraction.

Matthew E. May, in his book *The Laws of Subtraction*, makes the observation that "at the heart of every difficult decision lie three tough choices: What to pursue versus what to ignore. What to leave in versus what to leave out. What to do versus what to don't. I have discovered that if you focus on the second half of each choice—what to ignore, what to leave out, what to don't—the decision becomes exponentially easier and simpler … This is the art of subtraction: when you remove just the right thing in just the right way, something good usually happens."[86]

It's a strategic decision. When you choose to add something, subtract something first. I call it a stop-doing list. When you add something to your to-do list, subtract something, too.

Here's the point. We were not designed with infinite head space or bandwidth. We cannot be healthy if we only live by the laws of addition or even attraction. We are called to take the counterintuitive approach from time to time to learn the art of subtraction.

> This is the art of subtraction: when you remove just the right thing in just the right way, something good usually happens."

So the question when it comes to strategic stops is, if I add a strategic stop, what am I also subtracting?

Even if I choose, for example, to shape an existing team meeting into a strategically designed stop, what part of that normal meeting agenda will I want to exclude (or at least shorten) in order to make room for sharing and connecting and self-awareness?

If I am choosing to prioritize personal growth and development in my schedule, what am I replacing? What am I then going to subtract from my schedule in order to accommodate these new strategic stops?

If as a parent I'm going to choose to have no technology present during our family dinner times (turning them into strategic stops), what positive family experience will I replace it with? If no technology, then more of what? And how? And why?

And this one's a painful one for me: if I'm going to buy a new book, which book will I get rid of or give away? In my case, since I live in a small apartment, I definitely have limited space. So this, though painful, has been an important practice for me to engage in.

You get the idea.

The power of it is that with every subtraction, we open up the possibility for something new, something even better, something good, as Matthew May puts it. It's our choice.

One of my favorite classical composers is Claude Debussy. I still enjoy playing "Claire de Lune" on the piano. Debussy once wrote, "Music is the space between the notes."

If you know his music, you know that he is a master at spacing—intervals when no sound exists—even if only briefly. That silence and space between the notes serve to enhance the musicality and power of the notes. Imagine listening to a pianist or vocalist (or even speaker, for that matter—I've endured too many of them) who never stops—he or she plays/sings/speaks incessantly—with no breaks, no silence, no pause. How do you feel or react? It's simply exhausting, isn't it? Overwhelming. Easy to ignore and tune out. Our bandwidth gets used up before they're even done, so we check out. Effective composing is not just adding more notes to be played without rest or pause. It's learning how to subtract strategically, thoughtfully, emotionally. Space between the notes.

> The whole idea of the word stop is to cease from doing one thing in order to do another—something more strategic, empowering, and enhancing for those moments.

So make sure you're not just adding into your life plan strategic stops. The whole idea of the word stop is to cease from doing one thing in order to do another—something more strategic, empowering, and enhancing for those moments.

5. Are you embedding strategic stops into your personal and professional culture so you can practice them regularly and get better at them?

When I was a kid, practicing the piano for several hours every day after school, my dad would on occasion walk through the living room and, as he passed me by, say, "Remember, Greg, practice makes perfect." And then he'd walk on out of the room.

"Thanks, Dad. Great wisdom. You must have been awarded a PhD for that," I would sarcastically think to myself.

But as I became an adult, I realized that my dad was speaking truth. You simply can't get good at anything without regular, strategic practice. My piano teacher made sure my practice was strategic—"Just pounding on the keys, Greg, won't be helpful. Play every phrase separately. Memorize it. And then repeat it. Again and again. When you're away from the piano, close your eyes. Picture the notes. Then run your fingers over the surface in front of you playing those notes like you are at the piano keyboard. Repeat. Again and again. Take each page and learn it, memorize it. Then play the piece backward. Again." And on and on she went.

Now that's what real practice is. Strategic. Relentless.

When I was getting ready for a solo recital at the end of the summer after my first year in high school, I was practicing the piano eight hours every day, Monday through Friday. Four hours in the auditorium in the morning. Lunch break. And then four hours in the afternoon. Those piano pieces embedded themselves, every note of them, into my psyche. And eventually even into my dreams at night. Every note. So that years later, I could still play those pieces perfectly. I had successfully implanted them into my personal culture.

> Nothing of any consequence can be attained with excellence without practice, strategic development, and repetition.

Nothing of any consequence can be attained with excellence without practice, strategic development, and repetition.

Neuroscientists tell us that our brains expend a lot of energy when we're learning a new behavior or activity that demands concentration. A broad range of brain areas light up with energy as glucose and oxygen are increased to those spots. As we become more skilled at the task, however, our brains become more focused: we require only the essential brain regions and need increasingly less energy to perform that task. Once we have mastered a skill, only the brain areas directly involved remain active. In this way, learning a new skill requires more brainpower than a well-practiced activity.

So the more we practice something, the more efficient our brains become, utilizing less energy. The behaviors and activities become more natural to us.

My encouragement to you is to develop your own strategic stops and make them a regular, even natural, part of your life. It may be more difficult at first. You may not be used to carving out these kinds of intentional pauses in your life. But the good news is my dad was right. Practice does make perfect … or at least easier. And the more you practice these stops, the more efficient your brain becomes, and the more effective you become in managing your energy. It's a win-win.

So utilize these five important questions to evaluate your strategic stops:

1. Are your strategic stops helping you become more fully alive?
2. Are your strategic stops enhancing your essential human skills?
3. Are the boundaries of your strategic stops clearly defined?
4. With every strategic stop you initiate, what are you in turn subtracting from your schedule?
5. Are you embedding strategic stops into your personal and professional culture so you can practice them regularly and get better at them?

The great leadership pioneer Peter Drucker said, "You cannot manage other people unless you manage yourself first."

You are the beginning point.

But the satisfying thing is that as you develop yourself, as you become more human and more fully alive, like a rock tossed into a still pond, you will create ripple effects that ripple out wider and wider to inspire the people around you—your employees, teams, significant others, children, friends, neighborhood, and communities.

This is how the world can be changed for the good. You can do it. Let's do it!

Acknowledgements

In harmony with the latest neuroscience, I want to now take a swig of serotonin (the happy molecule that enhances mood, willpower, and motivation) by expressing deep gratitude and appreciation to people who made this book not only possible but also a reality. And if you're reading this, you will enjoy a mood booster with me. That's the way gratitude works. So I pause for this strategic stop for acknowledgment and recognition of these important people to my life and project.

To my wife and life partner, Shasta Nelson, my gratitude, appreciation, love, and passion know no bounds. Her continual support, encouragement, wisdom, suggestions, brainstorming sessions, editing, and reminders of who I am and what my purpose is and where my true value comes from energized and empowered me to write this book in a way that made it far better than I could have on my own. She is the queen of strategic stops and brings a level of joy and happiness into my life that words cannot adequately express.

To my three children and their significant others—Vaughn and Becky; Natalie, Geoff, and Dante; and Julian and Haidee. Again and again through the years, they've taught me the value of taking strategic stops for family time, meaningful conversations, adventures, and expanding experiences. They've been significant sounding boards for this book. Their unconditional love continues to keep me going.

To my parents—Paul and Barbara Nelson—who, though no longer with us, left me an enduring legacy of the value of strategic stops from childhood on that has inspired me and continues to shape my own purposeful pauses for myself and with those I love and serve.

My best friends—Paul Richardson and Bruce Elliot-Massarsky—whose deep and meaningful friendships through the years continue to encourage and uplift me in profound ways. They have been thought partners and emotional support for me in this project from beginning to end, and their love empowers me every day to soar into my potential.

To the people who have been a part of my Mastermind group—especially Nancy Larocca Hedley and Kris Carey during the last couple of years—consummate professionals who place high priority on personal and professional growth and development, who have held up the mirror to me many times in ways that have helped me see my truer and better self and how to live in that space more fully. This book wouldn't have happened as easily without their wisdom and cheerleading.

My editor—Lauren Bongard Schwarz—showered her professional and keen insight into my manuscript to make it a much better book. I am indebted to her for all her hard work, ideas, suggestions, and amazing expertise.

My book designer—Carla Green of Clarity Designworks—worked her creative magic on my book covers, internal layout, digital edition, and book production. Her wisdom in how to communicate my message in the most authentic and visually appealing way has been profoundly meaningful.

To all my Kickstarter backers—your faithful support to my book project, your pledges, your affirming encouragement, your excitement to see the finished product and share it widely—all of these gifts given to me so generously have kept me going. I'm thrilled that you finally are holding my book in your hands.

And lastly but not least, to my clients—the leaders, teams, organizations, and countless individuals through the years. It's difficult to adequately express thanks and gratitude to you for trusting me into your lives, for choosing to intersect our journeys with each other, in ways that have not only taught me so much about what it means to live fully alive but also what it takes. I hope that I have made as much of a difference to you as you have to me. My wish for you continues to be that you will make the bold and strategic choices to live fully alive and more fully human, wherever you are.

Endnotes

Prologue

1   I am indebted to Lynne Twist's telling of this ancient story gleaned from her long-term interactions with the indigenous people of South America and beyond. Lynne Twist, The Soul of Money: Transforming Your Relationship with Money and Life (W.W. Norton & Company, New York: 2017, 2003), pp. 167-169.

2   Maria Popova, "Hermann Hesse on Solitude, the Value of Hardship, the Courage to Be Yourself, and How to Find Your Destiny," https://www.brainpickings.org/2019/01/15/hermann-hesse-solitude-suffering-destiny/.

Introduction

3   Charlotte Lieberman, "Device-free Time Is Just As Important As Work-Life Balance," April 13, 2017, https://hbr.org/2017/04/device-free-time-is-as-important-as-work-life-balance.

4   Ibid.

5   Jennifer Lachs, "Why Silence Is Good For Your Brain," October 22, 2016, http://www.opencolleges.edu.au/informed/features/silence-good-brain/.

6   Archibald Hart, Adrenaline & Stress (Waco, Texas: Word Books, 1986) p. 22.

7   Ibid., p. 30.

8   Maria Popova, "Leisure, the Basis of Culture: An Obscure German Philosopher's Timely 1948 Manifesto for Reclaiming Our Human Dignity in a Culture of Workaholism," https://www.brainpickings.org/2015/08/10/leisure-the-basis-of-culture-josef-pieper/?fbclid=IwAR0MS227Z1zeaxGia9eD0bsweC4z0rbopUF8DjiF_Mlkkuzls6nl8CoPMME.

Strategic Stop 1

9   "Why Do We Sleep Anyway?" a study from the Division of Sleep Medicine of Harvard Medical School (http://healthysleep.med.harvard.edu/healthy/matters/benefits-of-sleep/why-do-we-sleep)

10 Alex Soojung-Kim Pang, Rest (Basic Books, NY, 2016), p. 140.

11 "Sleep, Learning, and Memory" A study from the Division of Sleep Medicine of Harvard Medical School, http://healthysleep.med.harvard.edu/healthy/matters/benefits-of-sleep/learning-memory

12 Quoted in Dr. Frank Lipman, "A Conversation with Arianna Huffington: The Sleep Revolution," Be Well. https://www.bewell.com/blog/a-conversation-with-arianna-huffington-the-sleep-revolution/.

13 Genesis 2:7, 21-22.

14 Genesis 1:14-19.

15 Dr. Jennifer Lachs, "Why Silence is Good For Your Brain," October 22, 2016, http://www.opencolleges.edu.au/informed/features/silence-good-brain/

16 Ibid.

17 Emma Seppala, The Happiness Track (HarperCollins Publishers, New York, NY: 2016), p. 111.

18 Rachel Moeller Gorman, "Health Hazard: Too Much Noise Is Bad For You," Women's Health Magazine, December 12, 2011, https://www.womenshealthmag.com/life/a19912853/peace-and-quiet/.

19   Timothy A. Pychyl, "The Personality of the Workaholic and the Issue of 'Self'", Psychology Today, March 20, 2010 (https://www.psychologytoday.com/blog/dont-delay/201003/the-personality-the-workaholic-and-the-issue-self)

20   Olga Mecking, "The Case for Doing Nothing," New York Times, April 29, 2019. https://www.nytimes.com/.../s.../the-case-for-doing-nothing.html.

21   Ibid.

Strategic Stop 2

22   Shawn Achor and Michelle Gielan, "Resilience Is About How You Recharge, Not How You Endure," June 24, 2016, https://hbr.org/2016/06/resilience-is-about-how-you-recharge-not-how-you-endure.

23   Kelvin Rodolfo, "What Is Homeostasis?" https://www.scientificamerican.com/article/what-is-homeostasis/#.

24   Shawn Achor and Michelle Gielan, "Resilience Is About How You Recharge, Not How You Endure," June 24, 2016, https://hbr.org/2016/06/resilience-is-about-how-you-recharge-not-how-you-endure.

25   A.A. Milne, The House at Pooh Corner (Dutton Children's Books, New York, NY: October 1988).

26   F.R.H. Zijlstra, M. Cropley, & L.W. Rydstedt, "From Recovery to Regulation: An Attempt to Reconceptualize 'Recovery from Work,'" Stress and Health, 30:244-252 (2014).

27   Christopher M. Barnes, "The Ideal Work Schedule, as Determined by Circadian Rhythms," January 28, 2015. https://hbr.org/2015/01/the-ideal-work-schedule-as-determined-by-circadian-rhythms.

28   Ibid.

29   F.R.H. Zijlstra, M. Cropley, & L.W. Rydstedt, "From Recovery to Regulation: An Attempt to Reconceptualize 'Recovery from Work,'" Stress and Health, 30:244-252 (2014).

Strategic Stop 3

30   Rick Hanson, "Just One Thing: Find Your North Star," Greater Good Magazine: Science-based Insights for a Meaningful Life, May 11, 2012.

31   Gregg Levoy, Callings: Finding and Following an Authentic Life (New York, New York: Three Rivers Press, 1997), 251.

32   Gregg Levoy, Ibid., p. 6.

33   Randy Pausch & Jeffrey Zaslow, The Last Lecture (New York: Hyperion, 2008) pp. 50–51.

Strategic Stop 4

34   Camille Sweeny and Josh Gosfield, "Secret Ingredient for Success," January 19, 2013, http://www.nytimes.com/2013/01/20/opinion/sunday/secret-ingredient-for-success.html?_r=1&

35   Fr. Kallistos, The Orthodox Way, p. 7. Crestwood, N.Y.: St. Vladimir's Orthodox Theological Seminary, 1979.

36   Martin Reeves, Roselinde Torres, and Fabien Hassan, "How To Regain the Lost Art of Reflection," Harvard Business Review, September 26, 2017, https://hbr.org/2017/09/how-to-regain-the-lost-art-of-reflection.

37   Ibid.

38   Travis Bradbury & Jean Greaves, Emotional Intelligence 2.0 (San Diego, CA: TalentSmart, 2009), p. 20-21.

39   "A single cell can grow 15,000 connections with its neighbors. This chain reaction of growth ensures the pathway of thought responsible for the behavior grows strong, making it easier to kick this new resource into action in the future." Ibid., p. 52.

40   Ibid., p. 52.

41   Ibid., p. 26.

42   Martin Reeves, Roselinde Torres, and Fabien Hassan, "How To Regain the Lost Art of Reflection," Harvard Business Review, September 26, 2017, https://hbr.org/2017/09/how-to-regain-the-lost-art-of-reflection.

Endnotes

43 Ibid.

44 Dan Ciampa, "The More Senior Your Job Title, the More You Need to Keep A Journal," Harvard Business Review, July 7, 2017, https://hbr.org/2017/07/the-more-senior-your-job-title-the-more-you-need-to-keep-a-journal.

45 Mike Erwin, "In A Distracted World, Solitude is a Competitive Advantage," Harvard Business Review, October 19, 2017, https://hbr.org/2017/10/in-a-distracted-world-solitude-is-a-competitive-advantage.

46 Thornton Wilder, Our Town (A Play in Three Acts) (A Perennial Classic. New York: Harper and Row, Publishers, Inc. 1968), p. 100.

Strategic Stop 5

47 Camille Sweeny and Josh Gosfield, "Secret Ingredient for Success," January 19, 2013, http://www.nytimes.com/2013/01/20/opinion/sunday/secret-ingredient-for-success.html?_r=1&.

48 Here is a helpful list of emotional vocabulary that is divided into Pleasant Feelings and Difficult/Unpleasant Feelings with subsections based upon themes of feelings. It's quite complete and very useful. http://www.psychpage.com/learning/library/assess/feelings.html

49 Bradberry and Greaves, Emotional Intelligence 2.0, p. 64.

50 Tom Deierlein, "Why Is US Army's AAR (After Action Review) Such A Powerful Leadership Tool?" August 9, 2014, LinkedIn. https://www.linkedin.com/pulse/20140809133352-404673-why-is-the-army-s-aar-after-action-review-such-a-powerful-leadership-tool/.

51 George Pratt and Peter Lambrou, Code to Joy. (San Francisco, California: Harper One, 2012). The seven self-limiting beliefs are: I am not safe, I am worthless, I am powerless, I am not lovable, I cannot trust anyone, I am bad, I am alone.

52 Ibid., p. 36.

Strategic Stop 6

53 Towers Perrin's Global Workforce Study.

54 "What Is Self-Determination Theory?" February 21, 2017, https://positivepsychologyprogram.com/self-determination-theory/.

55 Marcus Buckingham & Donald O. Clifton, Now, Discover Your Strengths (The Free Press, Simon & Schuster, Inc.: New York, NY, 2001) p. 131.

56 You can take the assessment by going directly to https://www.GallupStrengthsCenter.com or buying the book StrengthsFinder 2.0 and using the included ID code to gain access to the online test.

57 Buckingham & Clifton, Ibid., p. 137.

58 Gallup Strengths Center, https://www.GallupStrengthsCenter.com.

59 Arlene Taylor, "Adapting," from Realizations, Inc. http://arlenetaylor.org/practical-applications/brain-bent/7292-adaption-and-falsification-of-type.

60 See some of the research in Marianne Cooper, "For Women Leaders, Likeability and Success Hardly Go Hand in Hand," Harvard Business Review, April 30, 2013. https://hbr.org/2013/04/for-women-leaders-likability-a.

Strategic Stop 7

61 Shawn Achor, Gabriella Rosen, Kellerman Andrew Reece, Alexi Robixhaux, "America's Loneliest Workers, According to Research," Harvard Business Review, March 19, 2018, https://hbr.org/2018/03/americas-loneliest-workers-according-to-research?utm_medium=email&utm_source=newsletter_daily&utm_campaign=dailyalert&referral=00563&deliveryName=DM3097.

62 Amy C. Edmondson, The Fearless Organization (John Wiley & Sons: Hoboken, New Jersey, 2019), p. xiv.

63 Ibid.

64 Shasta Nelson, Frientimacy: How to Deepen Friendships for Lifelong Health and Happiness (Seal Press: Berkeley, California, 2016), pp. 30-45.

65   Charles Duhigg, "What Google Learned From Its Quest to Build the Perfect Team," New York Times, February 25, 2016. http://www.nytimes.com/2016/02/28/magazine/what-google-learned-from-its-quest-to-build-the-perfect-team.html.

66   Ibid.

67   Ibid.

68   Stephen R. Covey, The 7 Habits of Highly Effective People (Simon and Schuster: New York, New York, 1989), p. 30-31.

Strategic Stop 8

69   Abraham Joshua Heschel, The Sabbath (New York: Farrar, Straus and Giroux, 1951), p. 29.

70   Justin McCurry, "Japanese woman 'dies from overwork' after logging 159 hours of overtime in a month, The Guardian, Oct. 5, 2017, https://www.theguardian.com/world/2017/oct/05/japanese-woman-dies-overwork-159-hours-overtime.

71   Gay Hendricks, The Big Leap: Conquer Your Hidden Fear and Take Life to the Next Level (New York, New York: HarperCollins Publishers Inc., ePub edition, 2009), p. 166.

72   Ibid., p. 167.

73   Walter Bruggemann, The Sabbath As Resistance: Saying No to the Culture of Now (Louisville, KY: Westminster John Knox Press, 2014), p. 90.

Strategic Stop 9

74   Marianne Williamson, The Age of Miracles (Hay House Publishers, 2008) p. 48.

75   Howard Thurman, Deep Is the Hunger (Ravenio Books, 1951) Meditation #9.

76   Gallup, State of the American Workplace, "Executive Summary" (Gallup, Inc., 2017) p. 8.

77   Laurent Chevreux, Jose Lopez, and Xavier Mesnard, "The Best Companies Know How to Balance Strategy and Purpose," Harvard Business Review, November 2, 2017, https://hbr.org/2017/11/the-best-companies-know-how-to-balance-strategy-and-purpose.

78   Matthew 13:3-9.

79   Williamson, Ibid., pp. 48-49.

Conclusion

80   Irenaeus, Bishop of Lyon, France, 185 AD.

81   Rasmus Hougaard, Jacqueline Carter, Vince Brewerton, "Why Do So Many Managers Forget They're Human Beings?" Harvard Business Review, January 29, 2018, https://hbr.org/2018/01/why-do-so-many-managers-forget-theyre-human-beings.

82   Valerie Strauss, "The surprising thing Google learned about its employees — and what it means for today's students," The Washington Post, December 20, 2017, https://www.washingtonpost.com/news/answer-sheet/wp/2017/12/20/the-surprising-thing-google-learned-about-its-employees-and-what-it-means-for-todays-students/.

83   Ibid.

84   Monica Anderson and Jin Jin Jiang, "Teens, Social Media, and Technology 2018," Pew Research Center Internet and Technology, May 31, 2018, http://www.pewinternet.org/2018/05/31/teens-social-media-technology-2018.

85   Judith Shulevitz, "How the Sabbath Keeps Jewish People," Haaretz, April 2, 2010, https://www.haaretz.com/1.5099822.

86   Matthew E. May, The Laws of Subtraction: Six Simple Rules for Winning in the Age of Excess Everything (New York, New York: McGraw Hill, 2013), p. xii.

About the Author

Greg Nelson is a professional speaker, leadership and team strengths coach, and author of *The Strategic Stop*—a guide to creating purposeful pauses for reflection and connection in our always-on society. He is recognized as an expert in team and leadership culture transformation with an earned doctorate in personal and organizational effectiveness. He has worked with high-profile companies and nonprofits such as the Bill and Melinda Gates Foundation, Fitbit, Amazon, Walmart, Lyft, and American Express. He also consults with church organizations that are striving to stay relevant. He has delivered thousands of talks in his career as a pastor and then as a full-time corporate keynote speaker and coach, to both small audiences and those in the thousands. He is a father to three amazing adults and a grandfather to his first grandchild. He and his wife, Shasta, live in North Beach, San Francisco.

For more information about how to book Dr. Nelson to speak at your event or to work with your leaders and teams, go to his website, www.GregoryPNelson.com or email him at greg@gregorypnelson.com. You can also follow him on Facebook, LinkedIn, Twitter, and Instagram at @gregorypnelson.